Wildflowers of the Western Great Lakes Region

Wildflowers of the Western Great Lakes Region

James R. Wells
Frederick W. Case, Jr.
T. Lawrence Mellichamp

Foreword by Warren Herb Wagner

Cranbrook Institute of Science
Bulletin 63

Library of Congress Catalog Card No. 97-078035

ISBN 087737-042-7

Editing and composition by Merry M. Sisneros
Color work and printing by Brophy Engraving Company
Dust jacket design by Lisa Babbitt
Layout design by Lisa Babbitt and Merry M. Sisneros

Dedicated to the memory of Dr. Albert P. Ulbrich –
humanitarian, osteopathic physician, amateur botanist,
and long-time member of Cranbrook Institute of Science

About Dr. Ulbrich

To all who knew him, Albert P. Ulbrich, D.O., typified the health care professional. A dermatologist, he was acutely aware of the relationship between the plant sciences and the practice of medicine. Because the earliest physicians used herbal remedies, he recognized the need to learn plant identification as a precursor to curing illness. In doing so, he combined two of the great loves of his life.

Dr. Ulbrich's early enthusiasm for both plants and medicine took root in his native New Jersey and blossomed during his college days in West Virginia, but his pursuits extended well beyond those areas of expertise. His Birmingham, Michigan, office bore many examples of his woodworking and photography interests and skills: wildflower photographs hung on walls that he paneled with real wood and furniture handcrafted from cherry, black walnut, and other woods native to Michigan. Among his other activities were lectures for the Michigan Botanical Club and various medical conferences.

His late wife Wilba, a trained nurse, was always at his side supporting his efforts in the office, at home, and wherever else his passion for life took him. One such additional venue was Cranbrook Institute of Science where the Ulbrichs were members for many years and participated in numerous volunteer activities. Dr. Ulbrich is survived by three sons, two of whom followed in his footsteps as osteopathic physicians.

There is no doubt that Dr. Ulbrich added to the quality of human existence for all with whom he came into contact, not the least of whom are the scores of patients he treated pro bono each year. It is therefore fitting that this volume be dedicated to his life and work. The frontispiece photograph of Michigan Lily was taken on his property only a few miles from Cranbrook.

Contents

Foreword

What a wonderful idea – the Western Great Lakes flowering plants in beautiful color. The region is renowned for its variety of wildflowers. Hikers, fishermen, conservationists, naturalists, and botanists come from all parts of the United States and Canada to appreciate the floral display that occurs southward from May to November and northward from May to October. Species replace each other as the season progresses, starting with the delicate spring flowers and ending with the more robust varieties of fall. Our habitats thus change their flowering plants progressively throughout the season. The lover of nature goes back again and again to see the whole annual picture. What the authors of this book have done is to bring the variety of species from all seasons together, arranging them according to the typical habitats in which they are likely to be found. This fine assemblage of photographs will be of maximum value for learning the plants and for identifying them when they appear in their natural settings as well as a source of enjoyment in the bleakness of winter.

Our authors are all well known botanists, each having many years of experience with Great Lakes plants. Longtime friends of mine, they have all had connections with Cranbrook Institute of Science and at least some training at the University of Michigan in Ann Arbor. All have worked hard for conservation of our rare species and the preservation of natural areas. As teachers they are familiar with the problems of presenting details about plants to students and to the general public. This interest in communication, I'm sure, is responsible for their becoming expert photographers in order to illustrate their respective lectures and public programs.

When I think of the Great Lakes flora, I am amazed at the diversity of habitats, often in such close association that we can walk from one to the other over a short distance. From wet to dry, from open to shaded, these sites extend from river edges to lakes and ponds; to marshes, bogs, and fens; to swamps of all descriptions including coniferous and hardwood; to jack pine and other coniferous upland forests; to Oak-hickory and Beech-Sugar Maple forests; and to the very interesting open habitats – the oak openings and prairies. These together comprise an array of ecosystems so diverse that even their classification has been controversial.

Just as interesting as these more or less stable habitats are those that result from disturbance, natural or man-made. Surprisingly, many of our most interesting wildflowers occur under these conditions. The problem with such habitats is that they gradually transform into different habitats. For example, repeated burning may produce prairies, but if fire is kept out the site will transform into woods and the fascinating prairie wildflowers will disappear. The same is true for dune habitats which are, by their nature, constantly changing through the years. Finally the dunes may become "tamed" by natural succession and their peculiar wildflower prizes will then die out.

Along with its many geographically widespread species of wildflowers, common or rare, there are some that are known only from the Upper Great Lakes area. These include the gorgeous Lakeside Iris, the Huron Tansy, the Michigan Monkey Flower, and Pitcher's Dune Thistle. Especially interesting are those species that occur also in our Great Lakes area as outliers at long distances from their metropolises. A number of these are illustrated in this book.

The different combinations of shapes and colors of our wildflowers seem unlimited. Pendant bell-shaped flowers with bright orange, spotted colors (as in Michigan Lily, among our largest flowers); tight heads of tiny flowers with the middle flowers black and the peripheral flowers yellow-orange and petal-like (as in Black-eyed Susan); loose clusters of narrow bilateral pink flowers (as in Bergamot). The most brilliant red color is surely that of the spectacular Cardinal Flower of shady swamp margins and sometimes damp ditches. The most extraordinary shape and color combinations are shown in the illustrations of various species of native orchids.

Without doubt, this book will contribute much to the public knowledge and understanding of the plants that grow in the Western Great Lakes region, particularly with its organization of species by habitat. It will also serve as a continuous source of pleasure for its readers, introducing them to a world of beauty and enjoyment, our heritage of native wildflowers.

Warren Herb Wagner
September, 1997

Acknowledgements

The unique richness of the flora of the lakeshores, dunes, forests, wetlands, and prairies of the Great Lakes region intrigued us long before we first came together from our various backgrounds to start this book in 1974 at the instigation of James R. Wells. Through involvement with The University of Michigan Biological Station, The University of Michigan's Matthaei Botanical Garden in Ann Arbor, the Michigan Natural Areas Advisory Council, the Michigan Botanical Club, and the taking and teaching of various field courses during our careers, we have refined our sense of appreciation of the region – a debt we owe to all these organizations. Our approach in this text is the result of our individual and collective devotion to understanding, explaining, and preserving as much as possible of the natural world, and we are grateful to Cranbrook Institute of Science for allowing us to bring our project to reality.

No volume with such a wide scope of species diversification and geographical range of coverage can be successfully attempted without the assistance and cooperation of many people along the way.

We would like first to acknowledge our wives (Jan, Roberta, and Audrey, respectively) and families. The benefit of their forebearance during our collective 100 years and more of field work studying and photographing plants as well as the time needed to bring this project to its conclusion is appreciated more than words can express. Their encouragement is also to be acknowledged, for sometimes we felt overwhelmed by the task before us. The assistance of Roberta Case during the long sessions of selecting photographs and helping to clarify what we were trying to convey was especially valuable.

We are individually fortunate to have studied under Prof. Warren H. (Herb) Wagner, author of the foreword herein, who instilled in us the idea that plants can be fun, that sight is a faculty, and that seeing is an art. Other University of Michigan botanists to whom much credit is due are Professors Anton (Tony) Reznicek who assisted with identification of certain critical species and review of our material and Dr. Edward G. Voss whose instruction and research assistance proved invaluable. He further permitted the use of glossary definitions from his own acclaimed three-volume work, *Michigan Flora*. The friendship of these three colleagues is an added bonus to their professional expertise. The late Helen V. Smith also deserves mention. Her earlier guide, *Michigan Wildflowers*, was useful to us in learning the common flora of the region and is the source of line drawings used in Appendix 3.

We are thankful to the Nature Conservancy, various state and regional parks and nature preserves, and known and unknown individuals and institutions who made their lands available for our purposes. The saving and sharing of wild plants and natural areas is a collective effort and an act of generosity.

Although our process for selection of photographs for this book began with many thousands of slides, we nevertheless found it necessary to rely on other photographers for a few desired species. Mr. Thomas A. Friedlander, Dr. Anton Reznicek, Dembinsky Photo Associates, and Mr. Dan Hayes generously provided assistance in filling these gaps.

Actual production of the book would not have occurred without the generous support of the Hanes Fund and the family of Dr. Albert P. Ulbrich.

Our thanks go also to late Institute Director Dr. Daniel Appleman who provided the impetus for us to finish what we started and offered us encouragement and support along the way.

Finally, we must acknowledge the very significant contribution of Ms. Merry Sisneros, publications specialist at Cranbrook Institute of Science, who went far beyond her usual duties in bringing this book to completion. This included resurrecting the project from a long period of inactivity; participating in long sessions for selection of photos to be included; editing and otherwise facilitating preparation of copy; completing the layout; acting as travel agent for us three geographically distant authors; and coordinating the various stages of production. It was a labor of love, and we share the final splendor of publication with her.

James R. Wells
Frederick W. Case, Jr.
T. Lawrence Mellichamp

Wildflowers of the Western Great Lakes Region

Introduction

When the first white explorers came to the territory that would become the Great Lakes region, they found a vast wilderness of swamps, plains, forests, and fens – a complex mosaic of habitats unlike anywhere in eastern North America. The two-mile-thick glaciers that covered the region for hundreds of centuries had all retreated within the previous ten thousand years, leaving behind deep piles of sand and gravel interspersed with holes and sloughs filled with water. As the climate warmed further, plants began to migrate northward from their southern retreats. The earliest to arrive found homes in what must have been relatively barren terrain where they established themselves, grew, and enriched the soil with their organic products and remains. With time, additional species from many regions of North America joined or supplanted the pioneering species. Continuing climatic changes since the Ice Age have exerted survival pressures on these plants, eliminating some from the region, enhancing the growth of others, and permitting some species to persist only in the northernmost, colder parts of our region or westward in drier districts. The results of all these actions are the plant formations of the western Great Lakes region that we see today.

But the development of any plant association is complex, involving not only the events of the past but also the dynamic, continuing saga of history, existing competition, climate, and outside events acting upon the site. Understanding the complicated ecology of our region is a lifetime science unto itself. In a book such as this, we can only superficially suggest the intricacy of processes acting to create the habitats we see. But even a small knowledge of such forces can greatly enhance one's understanding, enjoyment, and appreciation of the natural beauty around us.

A habitat does not just happen. It results from a long series of interactions between various plants and the conditions on the site. The specific type of habitat that develops on a given spot depends upon many factors: the nutrients present; the water-holding capacity of the soil; latitude; prevailing winds; rainfall; topography; even the stage of development of the site. What is remarkable is that the mixtures of species that we recognize as familiar groupings are not everywhere the same but have, through time, sorted themselves into discrete associations that we can recognize repeatedly in different locations where all the right factors occur.

Ecologists have long found it convenient to name major plant associations by one or a few of the dominant or most numerous plants present as, for instance, Beech-Sugar Maple forest, cedar-swamp, or Jack Pine plains. But many more species occur in each association than those named. Beech-Sugar Maple forest may contain some Basswood (*Tilia americana*), Tulip-poplar (*Liriodendron tulipifera*), Canada Hemlock (*Tsuga canadensis*), several oak species, and other woody plants. Occasionally in our region, though, the Beech-Sugar Maple forest will consist almost entirely of those two species or Sugar Maple (*Acer saccharum*) alone. Whatever the mix, the presence of the dominant species tells us things about soil fertility and what other plants we may expect to find there. In the Beech-Sugar Maple forest association, the soil will be moderately fertile, and we can expect a glorious profusion of spring wildflowers including Spring-beauty, hepatica, trilliums, Dutchman's-breeches, and trout-lilies. In drier or less fertile sites or in wetter, more peaty locations, we find different species of wildflowers or different proportions of species in the mix. But each assemblage will, to some degree, appear with a given set of dominant species to form one of our familiar plant habitats. Within one climatic district, observant individuals soon learn what common plants to expect in the major habitats present and where to find the more interesting or challenging treasures.

Because of natural forces in a given district, as for instance the summer cooling and winter moderating effects of the Great Lakes locally or the drying effect of the Rocky Mountain rain shadow upon the Great Plains, many natural regions have rather specific boundaries. One might expect certain plants, therefore, to occur only within the region that best meets their needs. But such is not always the case. The precise needs of a given species may not be as obvious as what we think they are. Many plants characteristic of the treed fens and bogs of the Great Lakes region grow in the sopping wet beds of mosses there. One familiar with the species only in that habitat tends to assume the plant is a wetland species demanding much water. Yet, in the boreal forests of Canada, the same species is found not in the wet bog but in sunny, drier, upland soils. Not water, but rather the cool root temperatures provided by the constant evaporation of water from the wicking mosses allowed the plant to remain and survive in the bogs in a region that otherwise no longer met its basic needs.

Many of our herbaceous species do not compete well with taller or more aggressive plants and can succeed only in a specific, open, competition-free situation such as that at the wave-lap zone of a lake where constant wave action keeps the soil open and suitable or where high water tables favor that plant but eliminate most competitors. Such a species may occur today not only in these habitats but also in a number of man-made situations – borrow or gravel pits; sandfills; or newly cleared ditches that, at least for a while, mimic that plant's original habitat. Other species may persist on cliffs and rockslides where a specific exposure coupled with continuous erosion repeatedly creates freedom from competition under conditions acceptable to that species. Old fields of abandoned farmlands may provide a temporary home for prairie species. The lumber-era pattern of rapid cut, slash, and burn at the turn of the last century created much prairie-like, humus-free soil in what had been a forest habitat. Over the past half-century, numerous prairie species, especially those with easily windborne seeds, migrated far eastward into our region. Since about 1950, many of these species have become more rare or extinct here as forest redevelops on fallow lands. (See discussions under Rocky Outcrops, Cliffs, and Alvar and elsewhere in this book.)

Transition areas between climate zones commonly occur. Northern and southern species will mingle on the steep slopes of the Blue Ridge escarpment in North Carolina. Western species occur in prairie-like habitats, whatever their origin, in Ontario, Michigan, Ohio, Indiana, Wisconsin, and elsewhere. Northern species creep southward into suitable habitats where cool soils provide the proper environment for their roots to function. Southern species may find a niche in a more northern location if enough factors are suitable for their particular survival.

The western Great Lakes region is an extraordinary example of a biogeographical crossroads. Latitude; longitude; the influences of the largest bodies of fresh water in this hemisphere; the deep, well-drained, sand-gravely soils of glacial origin; the granitic Canadian Shield in northern Ontario, Michigan, Wisconsin, and Minnesota; the limestones of the Niagaran escarpment; the fertile sands and clay of the postglacial lacustrine deposits on lakeplain prairie – all affect what can grow here. The present Great Lakes themselves have created and continue to create majestic sand dunes, miles of shoreline habitat, marshes, ponds, and beaches, both sandy and rocky, that harbor myriad wildflowers. Some of these – such as Pitcher's Thistle, Dwarf Lake Iris, and Lake Huron Tansy – can be found only here. The unique conditions in the Great Lakes region support a more diverse flora than any other eastern region north of subtropical Florida.

There is yet another process in nature that must be considered to understand and appreciate fully the diversity of our native vegetation. We stated earlier that a habitat of a given type does not just happen. Rather the sorting out process consists of a complex yet somewhat predictable series of developments favoring different growth forms. Biologists refer to this as "plant succession."

For convenience, we can recognize two basic pathways: succession on dry bare rock or soil and succession in a body of water such as a large pond or small lake. Once we recognize these generalized pathways, we can usually see all succession in any habitat as a variation on one of them.

Succession on bare rock or sterile soil starts with lichens. These simple organisms, a symbiotic coupling of an alga and a fungus, grow on bare rocks or soil. As they grow, meet, and compete, they excrete wastes, carbon dioxide, and other products. Dew or rain, dissolving their carbon dioxide, creates weak acids that etch the rocks or release minerals from them. Where competing lichens overlap, lack of light kills the shaded lichen and the dead areas decay into water-holding humus. This, with environmental water, forms humic acids that also etch and dissolve the rock. In short, the presence and actions of the lichens move the habitat from an extremely hostile one of dry and moist extremes and temperature fluctuations (daytime absorption of the sun's heat versus the cold of nighttime radiation) to a slightly less hostile situation. As the lichens and their products accumulate, the environment becomes increasingly less suitable for the establishment of lichens and a better place for other plant propagules. In time, mosses can establish and succeed better than lichens, and a moss stage takes over.

In like manner, mosses change the habitat, increasing the humus and soil properties. Other factors, such as the freeze-thaw action of water in rock crevices that fractures off bits of rock, increase the depth and variety of the soil. Moss-eating organisms arrive, feed, excrete, and in other minute ways help build the soil. Eventually the mosses have created conditions their propagules cannot handle, but now various herbs may find enough foothold to establish. So, lichens give way to mosses; mosses give way to herbs, at first either large, aggressive weeds or, as seen in moist mossy sands, such showy wildflowers as Fringed Gentian, Lance-leaved Violet, and Dwarf Lake Iris.

The pioneer herbs, in turn, give way to grasses. Grasses spread both by seed and runners, soon forming strong sods that quickly exclude most other herbs. Eventually, better adapted sun-loving shrubs appear and spread by runners into vast mounds (observe any long-standing old field), shading out the grasses. The grassland becomes ever more a bed of competing shrubby mounds (Gray-twigged Dogwood [*Cornus formina*], sumac, blueberry, etc. in our region). Pioneer trees appear, often in shrubby thickets, on a bit of animal disturbed soil or at a pond's edge. Shrubland gradually gives way to a pioneer forest of sun-loving trees – Cottonwood (*Populus deltoides*), Red Maple (*Acer rubrum*), Silver Maple (*Acer saccharinum*), White Birch (*Betula papyrifera*), various oaks, Jack Pine (*Pinus banksiana*), Quaking or Trembling Aspens (*Populus tremuloides*) – and accumulation of humus (leafmold) accelerates.

More and more shade occurs as the pioneer trees increase their canopies. Soon the offspring of the pioneer species cannot tolerate the shade and humus created by their parents. New species whose seedlings tolerate the shade and humus appear. In parts of our region it may be a White Pine or a Beech-Sugar Maple forest. Shade tolerant species adapt their growth rate to the available light, do not attempt to use more food than they can produce, and mark time. Tree by tree, as the old forest trees die from whatever cause, one of these understory trees, in the light hole created, increases growth and grows up to fill the hole in the forest canopy. This can be seen so clearly at Hartwick Pines State Park in Michigan. Sugar Maple and beech succeed and take over the canopy from the White Pine (*Pinus strobus*), tree by tree. In the dense shade under these maples and beeches one can see a bed of tiny "seedlings" of the same, but some of those "seedlings" are 30, 40 or more years old. Once established in our region, the shade-tolerant Beech-Sugar Maple forest becomes stabilized with the offspring growing in its parent's shade. So long as the climate does not change perceptibly that forest, termed a climax formation, can continue indefinitely. While this is much oversimplified, all succession on normally dry sites is a variation on this basic pattern.

In ponds or lakes, because water can hold only a small proportion of the oxygen necessary for plant decay, the growth rate produces more material per season than can completely decay. What is left over, commonly termed "peat," accumulates on the bottom of the pond, gradually filling it. At first, floating species and bottom-dwelling aquatic plants colonize the edges and shallows. As more and more vegetation grows, organic matter accumulates, adding to the substrate. Upland sediments wash in and increase the bulk. Wherever there is sufficient sunlight to drive the food-making processes, plants grow. The more that grow, the more sediments; the more sediments the more peat. More peat means more shallows, and more shallows more plants. In the shoreline areas of shallowest water, emergent plants – reeds, sedges, and grasses – appear. These plants with tough runners bind the peat into weakly submerged mats that the emergents soon colonize.

Seen from above, a well developed bog lake is zoned like a target with a bullseye: a deep center of open water; then a zone of submerged aquatics; a zone of waterlily-type, floating vegetation; an emergent sedge mat; a moss mat; a shrub zone of specialized bog shrubs; and nearest the original shore on the oldest accumulated peat, a tree zone often of spruce and Tamarack (*Larix laricina*), sometimes called Larch. As each zone develops and grows toward the center of the lake, the margins begin to shrink. Eventually the lake becomes filled, all open water disappears, and for a while there is a clearing, a floating mat of moss and plants in the center of what had been a lake. Because peat is strongly acidic, it is a preservative. As more peat accumulates, less plant matter can decay and peat accumulation snowballs.

Each stage, like every other stage in any succession, has specialized, highly adapted species found only there. In peat bogs, characteristic herbs include pitcher-plants, sundews, and many orchids. Woody shrubs include Leatherleaf, cranberry, Highbush Blueberry, Poison Sumac, and Michigan Holly. Long after the open water is gone, succession continues. Finally the mat is compacted and covered by shrubs and eventually by a bog forest of Tamarack and spruce. If it is a mineral fen with less acid peat, additional species may appear and the forest may be called a cedar-swamp.

The general process of bog development may take hundreds of years. Slow drainage in a wetland tends to retard peat accumulation, add minerals, and delay the process. Sometimes, though, open water closes surprisingly fast. We have seen the open water area of one bog pond at Hartwick Pines State Park decrease four-fold in only about 50 years.

As each stage changes, so do the inhabitants – plant and animal. Eventually a once open bog mat, haven of pitcher-plants, Rose Pogonia, Grass Pink and fringed-orchids, becomes a dark forest of bog conifers in which none of those plants can survive. Other species adapted to the new conditions colonize and flourish. If sufficient peaty material accumulates to raise the substrate high enough above the water table, new successional stages resemble those described above for dryland succession. In theory at least, eventually the typical regional climax formation will appear. Since size, exposure, and depth of the lake all affect the rate of succession, in our region almost every bog is unique in being at a slightly different stage in its development. This succession has been proceeding since glacial retreat 10,000 years ago. The last of the glacially-formed lakes may fill in the coming century. Disturbance, drainage, fire, or drought has the effect of altering the successional pattern. Usually this means a backing up to an earlier stage and redevelopment of the original pattern. Drainage, however, allows complete decay of the peat substrate and may cause devastating changes to bog vegetation.

Finally, let us restate that in any given region, what is growing on the land at a given moment depends upon all of the climatological, geological, hydrological, and historical conditions at that spot *and* the stage of succession of that site. For each stage has its own unique occupants (species), therefore finding plants is, in part, a matter of reading the landscape. With knowledge, a sense of exploration, and an observant eye, you can quickly learn what general species should be present and what rarities might appear.

So, welcome to the western Great Lakes region. Notice the changes as you travel over the landscape and throughout the seasons. There is wonder and life everywhere you look. The water and the land intermingle to create a wonderful array of habitats. The history of this land, from the creation of the earth to the Ice Age glaciers, from the original Native Americans to the Voyageurs to the lumberjacks and farmers to the modern industrialist – all have influenced this region. The naturalist and outdoors person, the sport hunter, and the everyday citizen today marvel at the beauty and variety here. Most would wish to maintain and preserve as much as we can.

We want this book to aid the beginner in identifying our wildflowers and hope the clarity of the photographs and a word or two of text will help. But more than that, we want to celebrate our wondrous and regrettably shrinking heritage in the hope of fostering appreciation for the rich treasure that is ours to enjoy if we don't carelessly let it slip away.

Using This Book

In this book, we use the term "wildflower" in the broad sense of especially showy or particularly interesting plants. Included are a few flowering shrubs that produce striking blossoms or brilliant fruits, but flowering trees are excluded. We have tried to put species into the context of recognizable habitats and to explain something of the nature of each. This is an approach rarely taken in a wildflower book.

Wildflowers of the Western Great Lakes Region is intended primarily for beginners interested in becoming acquainted with our rich wildflower heritage rather than professional botanists. As previously stated, this book is organized into chapters by habitats. Within each habitat, individual species are arranged, in so far as possible, from earliest to latest time of blooming. But habitats are not stable, as described in this Introduction, and bloom times can vary within a region depending on latitude, season, and local weather conditions. So the resulting order is necessarily somewhat subjective. However, we judge the potential benefits of such an organization to a novice more compelling than its inherent limitations. Species more recognizable in fruit than flower are placed according to that aspect of their seasonal cycle.

To provide maximum space for photographs within the layout, we have elected to omit plant names under each picture. Rather the text provided for each one in almost every instance occurs directly adjacent to the picture. In the few cases where this was not possible, the text will be found no further from the photo than the facing page, and the order of the text blocks always mirrors that of the photo order on those facing pages. Photo credits are indicated as photographer initials at the lower right corner of each photo. Initials represent the following:

jrw	James R. Wells
fwc	Frederick W. Case, Jr.
tlm	T. Lawrence Mellichamp
taf	Thomas A. Friedlander
aar	Anton A. Reznicek
bg/dba	Barbara Gerlach/Dembinsky Photo Associates 1995 ©
gm/dba	Gary Meszaros/Dembinsky Photo Associates 1995 ©

In order to provide accurate descriptions of the plants, we have used basic botanical terminology, wherever possible accompanied by an explanation. In addition, a comprehensive glossary of terms can be found in the back of the book. We have chosen to omit the botanical authority from the Latin species names as these are generally of use only to specialists and may be found in more advanced books. We have also chosen to use English measurements as they remain the most widely understood. Plant families represented as common names in the text may be found in Appendix 1 in their full Latin expression. While there is no taxonomic key, we do provide in Appendix 2 a listing of plants by flower color as an aid to identification.

For purposes of consistency, we have used the following authorities:

For scientific names of plants other than the Orchid Family:

Voss, Edward G. 1996. Michigan Flora. Cranbrook Institute of Science & University of Michigan Herbarium. 3 vol.

For scientific names of plants in the Orchid Family:

Case, Frederick W., Jr. 1987. Orchids of the Western Great Lakes Region. Cranbrook Institute of Science Bulletin 48, Bloomfield Hills, Michigan. xxi + 251 pp.

Common names, by definition, are not dictated by an authority but rather reflect usage. They therefore can vary widely for the same species, even within a given geographical area. The common names appearing in this book are those most widely used and/or recognized within the western Great Lakes region and not necessarily those listed in standardized botanical texts. To distinguish the common names of covered species within the text, we have elected to capitalize them.

For distributional ranges:

Fernald, Merritt Lyndon. 1950. Gray's Manual of Botany. Ed. 8. American Book Company, New York. lxiv + 1632 pp.

Other references include:

Barnes, Burton V. and Warren H. Wagner, Jr. 1981 Michigan Trees. The University of Michigan Press, Ann Arbor, Michigan. 384 pp.

Gleason, Henry A. 1952. The New Britton and Brown Illustrated Flora of the Northeastern United States and Adjacent Canada. New York Botanical Garden, New York. 3 vol.

Meyer, Joseph E. 1934. The Herbalist. Hammond Book Company. Hammond, Indiana. 399 pp.

Smith, Helen V. 1966. Michigan Wildflowers. Cranbrook Institute of Science Bulletin 42, Bloomfield Hills, Michigan. xii + 468 pp.

Wherry, Edgar T. 1935. "Distribution of North American Pitcherplants" in Illustrations of North American Pitcherplants by Mary Vaux Walcott. Smithsonian Institute, Washington, D.C. 34 pp.

Deciduous Forest

The deciduous forests of eastern North America comprise a vast and complex series of woodlands resulting from the influences of latitude and longitude as well as geological factors such as glaciation, base rock formations, mineral content, elevation, and mountain orientation.

Presenting a green aspect in summer and showy colors in the fall, the deciduous forest ranges from northern Florida to eastern Texas and northward well into the northern Great Lakes States and Ontario. In the southeastern U.S. and southern portions of our region, the forest composition is almost exclusively deciduous species. The deciduous forest in the north of our region, however, is a transition zone between the northern coniferous forests and the deciduous forest of the south of the region. Thus it features a mixture of evergreen and deciduous trees.

Most plant communities on a given site are transitory. They develop where conditions for the seedlings of the species in that community can establish and subsist for a while. But as the plants mature, they create conditions of shade, humus development, and competition that prohibit their own seedlings from establishing and competing with them. Their offspring fail to establish or survive. But other species, adapted to the conditions the first group have produced, enter, establish, and eventually take over the area and, through competition and natural attrition, replace the previous plant community. Thus there is succession of plant communities on one site until a stage is reached in which seedlings of the plants tolerate the conditions their parents create and thus are able to persist. Such a stabilized community is termed a "climax formation." With each successional change, most of the wildflowers present are also replaced by other species because each wildflower species is adapted to only limited sets of conditions. The rate of changeover from one stage to another is not uniform. Temperatures, soils, slope, fertility, moisture – all influence the rate of change and the makeup of the mature stage when developed.

The deciduous forest tends to be a climax formation – that is, one capable of maintaining itself on the same site indefinitely once established, given no dramatic climate change.

In the south of our region, beech, Sugar Maple, Red Maple, Tulip-tree and various hickories and oaks dominate on the uplands. In the floodplains grow, or did grow before the advent of diseases, American Elm (*Ulmus americana*), Slippery Elm (*Ulmus rubra*), and several species of ash. Besides the dominant trees, smaller understory trees abound – Flowering Dogwood (*Cornus florida*), Alternate-leaved Dogwood (*Cornus alternifolia*), Redbud (*Cercis canadensis*), Red Mulberry (*Morus rubra*), Ironwood (*Ostrya virginica*), Blue Beech (*Caprinus caroliniana*) and others – as well as a host of shade tolerant shrubs. Among the most important such shrubs in our region are Spicebush (*Lindera benzoin*) and Red Elderberry (*Sambucus pubens*). For the most part, these plants grow on fertile, loamy, neutral soils that contain a distinct upper layer of decomposed matter that aids in regeneration.

Northward in our region, the deciduous forest, sometimes called the Appalachian Upland Forest, prevails, perhaps in a somewhat modified form. Here beech and most frequently Sugar Maple dominate the mature forest, sometimes almost to the exclusion of other species. Individual White Pines, a subclimax dominant, may persist in small numbers for many years, long after climax forest has covered most of the land. West of Lake Michigan, beech drops out abruptly, but Basswood, a very scattered species in the east of the area, becomes one of the forest dominants closer to the treeless prairies. In cool ravines and on north-facing hillsides, Canada or Eastern Hemlock, a shade-tolerant conifer, occurs as scattered trees or dense groves. In moist districts, the evergreen shrub Canada Yew (*Taxus canadensis*) may form dense thickets unless browsed out of existence by over-abundant deer.

The northern portion of this forest is both somewhat uniform in its resident wildflowers and quite variable locally. Some wildflower species occur throughout the mixed deciduous forest wherever suitable soils or conditions exist. Others characteristically occur in certain temperature ranges only. Taking advantage of the warming effect of the lakes in winter upon the eastward flowing air, essentially southern species tend to follow the lea shores of our Great Lakes, occurring in our region north of their general range. To a lesser degree southern pockets occur in Ontario along Lake Huron as well. As a general rule, the farther north one goes in the Great Lakes region, the fewer species present and the more uniform the forest appears.

Wildflowers that carpet the mixed deciduous forests fall into two categories – the spring ephemerals and the full season species. Spring ephemerals, by far the largest group commonly considered as "spring wildflowers," grow in bright light. Their flower buds,

formed the previous season, lie dormant until after spring frosts cease. Almost overnight, the plants expand their leaves and open their flowers. Upon pollination, the flowers decline and the plant goes into a photosynthetic "super gear." In a few short days or weeks, before the canopy of leaves robs them of light, these plants make and store enough food to produce both seeds this season and the flower buds for next year. Characteristically they demonstrate underground storage organs such as bulbs, tubers, and corms. As the tree leaves develop and reduce the light below, the plants become dormant until the next spring. Trout-lilies, Dutchman's-breeches, and Squirrel-corn exemplify this group.

Another set of deciduous forest herbs are more shade tolerant and continue to flourish as shade develops, maintaining their leaves and growth throughout most of the season. They include various ferns, Jack-in-the-pulpit, violets, and trilliums.

While the most species-diverse deciduous forest occurs south of the Great Lakes, forest in our region is rich in wildflower species. Many of these species are quite showy and likely the best known of our wildflowers.

Harbinger-of-spring
Erigenia bulbosa
Carrot or Parsley Family

One of the first of the many early wildflowers deemed "harbingers of spring" to bloom, this diminutive species is barely discernible in the leaf litter of the rapidly warming forest floor. A low and delicate perennial, Harbinger-of-spring produces tiny, umbrella-like clusters of flowers and small leaves that strongly suggest its relationship to carrots, dill, parsley, and its hundreds of other family members.

The black stamens of the tiny flowers contrast strongly with the white petals, providing the basis for another common name for this wisp of a plant, Salt-and-pepper.

Ranging from New York west to Michigan, Missouri, and Wisconsin, Harbinger-of-spring can flower as early as February and as late as April depending on latitude and may sometimes be found flowering under light snow cover.

Snow Trillium
Trillium nivale
Lily Family

Snow Trillium, a tiny jewel among early spring wildflowers, reaches a height of no more than 6 inches. It produces bluish-green, blunt-tipped leaves and small white flowers, in many ways miniatures of the more familiar large-flowered Large White Trillium. It flowers in late March or, in the northern part of its range, early April. Though Snow Trillium is rare and local, individual colonies can number in the thousands. Favoring floodplains and bottomlands near stream banks in our region, Snow Trillium is present only locally on specific river drainages in Michigan and Wisconsin but more widespread on Minnesota and Illinois loess soils. Also found in western Pennsylvania south to Kentucky and Missouri, Snow Trillium plants are easily overlooked in bloom. The plants wither by mid-June.

14

Sharp-lobed Hepatica
Hepatica acutiloba
Buttercup Family

Early to bloom with clusters of variously colored flowers, Sharp-lobed Hepatica is one of the most familiar of spring wildflowers. Flowering from March to early May, its blossoms range in color from pale to dark, from white to pink to rose to purple with a crown of tiny green pistils at the center. These color variations are on petal-like sepals as true petals are absent. Plants grow as clumps from the crown, like strawberry, and spread largely by ant-dispersed seeds. The three-lobed leaves are partially evergreen and liver-shaped. According to the medieval Doctrine of Signatures, their shape indicated supposed effectiveness in treating liver ailments.

Found throughout the eastern United States from Missouri and Minnesota south to Alabama and Georgia, this species likely occurs in non-acid soil that is rich and loamy.

Twinleaf
Jeffersonia diphylla
Barberry Family

This delightful spring wildflower gets its common name from the pair of triangular leaflets atop each leaf stalk, clusters of which arise from the underground crown of this low perennial. The Latin name commemorates our third president. In April and May, white flowers resembling those of Bloodroot emerge on separate stems among the leaves, typically with 8, 1-inch petals that last only a few hours to a day or so depending on temperature and wind. Distinctive pear-shaped capsules with pointed tops follow the flowers.

With a distribution range from New York and southern Ontario west to Wisconsin and Iowa and south to Alabama, Twinleaf usually lasts well into the season, the paired leaves maturing to a spread of 4 to 6 inches.

Narrow-leaved Spring-beauty
Claytonia virginica
Purslane Family

Broad-leaved Spring-beauty
Claytonia caroliniana
Purslane Family

Sending up their first flowers on the earliest warm days of spring, March to May depending on latitude, Spring-beauties arise from marble-sized underground tubers. Sprawling clusters of lax stems 5 to 8 inches tall bear single pairs of fleshy opposite leaves, narrow and tapering in one and wider and shorter in the other as the common names imply. Flowers of both species have 5 satiny, almost shimmering petals that display varying degrees of darker veining.

The veins of the narrow-leaved species may or may not be deep pink while those of the broad-leaved form are more often deep pink on deeper colored lavender-pink petals that are more

deeply cupped. Under ideal conditions in rich woods or on mowed lawns, Spring-beauty can create a virtual carpet of flowers an acre or more in size. Soon after the forest canopy leafs out, however, both species disappear entirely from the forest floor.

Longer stemmed and more sprawling in habit, Narrow-leaved Spring-beauty occurs only in the southern portion of the Great Lakes region while Broad-leaved Spring-beauty grows only in the northern half of the area. They mingle deep into the Southeast along the Appalachian Mountains.

Bloodroot
Sanguinaria canadensis
Poppy Family

A perennial that grows 4 to 12 inches tall, Bloodroot produces irregularly palmately-lobed leaves. Each flower blooms on a separate leafless stalk partially encircled by an unfolding leaf. With 8 to 12 white petals each 1 to 2 inches long, the blossoms of Bloodroot are extremely short-lived. Depending on weather, they can last from one to several days. Flowering occurs primarily in April, but leaves persist beyond the appearance of pointed seed pods that ripen by mid-summer. Extracts of the underground stems of Bloodroot find use today in the treatment of skin cancer and as an anti-plaque ingredient in toothpaste.

Bloodroot derives its name from the blood-red fluid produced in its fleshy underground stem and leaves. Used by Native Americans as a dye, a medicine, and a poison, the fluid will stain human skin orange.

Bloodroot ranges across Nova Scotia, Quebec, and Manitoba south to Florida and Texas.

Dutchman's-breeches
Dicentra cucullaria
Fumitory Family

Squirrel-corn
Dicentra canadensis
Fumitory Family

Dutchman's-breeches and Squirrel-corn often grow together in the rich soil of the forest floor. Delicate plants that die down by late May or early June, both feature finely dissected, fern-like leaves in grayish-green mounds 8 to 10 inches tall. Flower stalks rise above the mounded foliage producing nodding flowers in April. The creamy white flowers of Dutchman's-breeches have yellow tips and 2 outward spreading spurs resembling inflated pantaloons – the source of its common name. More fragrant, Squirrel-corn's white flowers are rounded at the base and resemble those of the horticulturally popular Bleeding-heart to which both are related.

Below ground, Dutchman's-breeches features a scaly, central white bulb while Squirrel-corn has small, widely separated yellow tubers that resemble corn kernels and provide the basis for its common name. The leaves of the two are virtually indistinguishable. Both plants range from Quebec to Minnesota south to Tennessee and Missouri.

fwc

Large White Trillium
Trillium grandiflorum
Lily Family

The showiest of all trilliums, Large White Trillium is locally abundant in most of our region. Typically found in massive colonies in rich, somewhat acid upland woods of southern Ontario, northern Michigan, Wisconsin, and northern Minnesota, it is less common and more local in Ohio, Indiana, and Illinois.

This erect, unbranched perennial can reach heights of 18 to 24 inches in vigorous colonies. A single whorl of 3 leaves tops the stem. The flower stalk emerges from the center of the whorl and bears a single blossom with 3 large petals. Quite variable in form, the flowers can have narrow or broad petals in a range of color from white to pink, all fading to a dull purple pink as they age. Sometimes these old pink flowers are mistaken for the red Wake-robin trillium. Double petaled forms with 30 or more petals also exist as do deformed green and white striped blossoms. Although showy, the latter are actually infected with a disease transferred by leaf hoppers.

Large White Trillium flowers between April and June in the Great Lakes region. Increasingly popular for gardens, if grown from seed it demands extreme patience as the required time from seed to flowering is about 7 years.

Many states protect Large White Trillium from collection on public land without a permit. Flowering-sized plants purchased for gardens should be propagated by a nursery, not collected from the wild.

Wake-robin; Stinking Benjamin
Trillium erectum
Lily Family

Widespread in the east from Newfoundland to Georgia, Wake-robin is local or absent in our region, occupying only isolated pockets in southern Ontario, the Michigan "thumb," central and northern Michigan, and the Cumberland Plateau in eastern Ohio. This typical trillium plant bears rather flat flowers from April to early June, its wide, spreading, pointed-ovate petals usually dark maroon or chocolate-red fading to dull purple-brown. White or pale yellow forms occur rarely.

Several common names for this species have interesting derivations. Wake-robin implies a comparison of the flower color to that of a robin's breast and it's blooming is said to signal that bird's return from the South. Both Stinking Benjamin and Wet Dog Trillium allude to the fetid odor of the flowers at close range, and Birthwort reflects the Indian belief that the plant dulls the pain of childbirth.

Toadshade; Sessile Trillium
Trillium sessile
Lily Family

The species name "sessile" in botany denotes that one organ is attached to another without a stem. In contrast to the Large White Trillium, the flowers of this trillium "squat" directly on the leaves. Its common name Toadshade derives from the umbrella-like, mottled green leaf cluster. The purpose of the mottling is unknown but some believe it evolved to help camouflage the plant from grazing animals including herbivorous insects. An early spring bloomer, Toadshade stands 4 to 10 inches tall and bears maroon brown or greenish petals that do not spread but remain erect like a bud.

Preferring rich limestone soils, Toadshade ranges from southern Michigan through Ohio and Illinois into Missouri, south to Alabama and east to Virginia, often in great abundance.

White Trout-lily
Erythronium albidum
Lily Family

Yellow Trout-lily
Erythronium americanum
Lily Family

The mottled, elongated leaves of the trout-lilies, resembling the shape and coloration of a trout's back, make them easy to identify and provide the basis for their "fishy" common name. Each leaf of these almost stemless perennials grows from a small bulb that may be as much as 7 inches underground. Working themselves deeper into the ground each year, the bulbs eventually use most of their energy getting the leaf to the surface. Hence, only a small percentage of individuals in a large colony may bloom in a given year. Following flowering, the bulbs send out underground shoots on which new bulbs form, thus producing extensive colonies.

Trout-lilies often carpet open woods from late March to June. Opening only in bright sunlight, the single, lily-like flowers with reflexed petals nod at the ends of their flower stalks for only a short time before giving way to marble-sized seed pods. As the pods mature, their increasing weight pulls them to the ground where they open and release their seeds. By early summer, even the leaves wither and disappear.

Rare or local in our region, White Trout-lily occurs in rich, upland woods or on river banks. Spreading less than the yellow form, it is a more southern and western species. Yellow Trout-lily is much more common throughout our area. The two may grow together, but the colonies tend to remain separate. The alternate names Dogtooth-violet and Adder's-tongue allude respectively to the fang-like shape of the white bulb and the protruding reddish or orange cluster of stamens.

Wild-ginger
Asarum canadense
Birthwort Family

Wild-ginger is usually identified by its hairy, heart-shaped leaves that can provide a bright green ground cover on the forest floor in summer. Its dark purple to reddish-brown flowers appear in April and May resting inconspicuously on the ground between the leaves. Said to be pollinated by gnats or slugs, the solitary flowers exhibit numerous variations in shape with 3 long sepals spreading out from a cup-shaped center or sometimes folding backward from the central opening.

Wild-ginger is a rampant spreader with creeping underground stems. A large patch, in fact, may be a single plant or "clone." The stems and shallow rhizomes in particular emit a ginger-like odor, and the rhizome reportedly can be candied and used as a confection.

This early wildflower typically occurs in rich, moist woods. It grows from Canada's Gaspé Peninsula and Quebec through North Carolina and Kentucky in the South.

Virginia "Bluebell"
Mertensia virginica
Borage Family

Nodding clusters of trumpet-shaped flowers characterize this fleeting spring charmer. Reaching heights of 18 to 24 inches, Virginia "Bluebell" features ovate, hanging leaves that may appear wilted. One of the first spring plants to die down completely, it flowers from late March to early June, the 1-inch flowers unfolding a few at a time atop a slender stalk. The buds and young flowers are pink but mature flowers are pale blue, the color difference apparently the result of a change from an acidic internal chemistry to a more alkaline one.

Virginia "Bluebell" grows in rich woods and floodplain forests. Found as far north as New York and southern Ontario, it extends south to South Carolina and Alabama and west to Arkansas and Kansas.

Rue-anemone
Anemonella thalictroides
Buttercup Family

This delicate, spring-flowering perennial produces 6- to 8-inch plants from small, starchy, tuberous roots that resemble sweet potatoes. Also called Windflower because it moves with the slightest breeze, Rue-anemone has leaves divided into 3-lobed leaflets, each 1/4 to 1/2 inch across and borne on a short stalk. Above the leaves is a group of white leaf-like bracts that form the base for an umbrella-shaped cluster of white flowers. Like many other members of the Buttercup family, it lacks petals but has showy sepals.

Rue-anemone usually grows in discrete clumps in rich open woodlands. Found principally in the northeastern United States, it occurs only in the southern portion of the Great Lakes region.

Jack-in-the-pulpit
Arisaema triphyllum
Arum Family

A striking arched hood makes Jack-in-the-pulpit among the easiest of the spring-flowering species to recognize. The fleshy-stemmed plants typically reach 1 foot in height but may be twice that tall given optimal growing conditions. The "pulpit" is actually a modified leaf inside of which is a spike of many tightly clustered flowers, the "Jack." The flowers are either male, producing pollen, or female, producing a large cluster of bright red berries, but not both. A specific plant will produce male flowers when young and have 1 leaf with 3 leaflets. As the plant matures in a suitable habitat, it can change to female with 2 leaves of 3 leaflets each. Given excess shade or a decrease in the nutrient supply, the plant will revert to male as pollen production requires less energy.

Jack-in-the-pulpit arises from an underground tuber that contains numerous oxalic acid crystals. If the tuber is bitten into, these crystals cause swelling and severe pain in the mouth. Color variations in the hood include stripes or patches in varying degrees of purple, green, and white. Flowering occurs in April and May with leaves maturing at approximately the same time, and oval clusters of shiny red berries are characteristic in the fall.

One of our most wide-ranging woodland species, Jack-in-the-pulpit occurs throughout eastern North America in moist woods.

25

Two-leaved Toothwort
Dentaria diphylla
Mustard Family

Typical of southern deciduous forests, Two-leaved Toothwort is an unbranched perennial that tends to grow in large masses. Plants average 4 inches tall in leaf and 6 to 8 inches in flower. As both its Latin (*diphylla*) and common names denote, each plant has only two leaves, each a unique green with lighter veins. The leaves have toothed margins and are divided into 3 leaflets. Between April and June, a few small white flowers appear on short individual stalks off the main stem, changing to pale pink as they mature.

Two-leaved Toothwort reproduces by seeds and underground stems. Its crisp rootstock is said to be edible, imparting a mustard or peppery flavor. Found in rich woods only as far west as southern Ontario and Michigan in the Great Lakes area, it can tolerate shade but requires constant moisture to flourish.

Pink Spring Cress
Cardamine douglassii
Mustard Family

Another member of the Mustard Family, Pink Spring Cress displays 4-petaled pink to deep pink or rarely white flowers as early as late April extending through May. The flowers occur at the tops of the 6- to 8-inch plants in clusters of few to many blossoms and exhibit the 2 short and 4 long stamens characteristic of its family. The stems of Pink Spring Cress tend to be hairy and arise from creeping underground roots that can form large colonies in rich wet woods and calcareous bottomlands. Like many of its family members, Pink Spring Cress is edible. The slightly bitter or peppery tasting plants can provide an interesting flavor in salads.

Found in the North from Connecticut across lower Ontario into Wisconsin, Pink Spring Cress extends as far south as Virginia, Tennessee, and Missouri.

26

Bellwort

Uvularia grandiflora
Lily Family

Bellwort is distinctive among early wildflowers in having flowering occur before its stem and leaves are mature, giving the 1- to 2-foot plants a wilted appearance at the top. A slender perennial with forking stems, it grows from a short, fleshy rootstock. Leaves up to 5 inches long surround the stem (i.e. are perfoliate), and solitary, 2-inch yellow flowers resembling bells hang beneath the leaves. Flowering occurs from April through early June.

An inhabitant of upland woods, low floodplain woods, and thickets, Bellwort occurs from Quebec to the Dakotas in the north and south to Georgia, Alabama, Arkansas, and Oklahoma.

Showy Orchis

Galearis spectabilis
Orchid Family

Among our native orchids, Showy Orchis is somewhat misnamed as it is rather inconspicuous and not nearly so "showy" as others in its family. Because it blooms at the height of the spring wildflower season, it is perhaps better known. Between large ovate leaves at or just above the ground, short, often stubby, flower spikes emerge and bear several flowers with a conspicuous white lip and pink to mauve sepals and petals that form a hood.

In the Great Lakes region, Showy Orchis reaches its flowering peak in mid-May to June when the forest leaves have reached about three-quarters of their full size. It can be locally abundant in varying types of deciduous forests but more commonly grows as scattered plants or in small colonies from Quebec, Ontario, and Minnesota south to Missouri, Georgia, and Alabama.

Bishop's-cap
Mitella diphylla
Saxifrage Family

Small, intricate flowers and a pair of stem leaves characterize this woodland species. Flowering stems a foot or more tall produce numerous quarter-inch, cup-shaped white flowers in April and May. Each of the 5 petals resembles a herringbone giving the entire blossom the appearance of a snowflake. Halfway up the stem are 2 opposite leaves, triangular in shape and at right angles to the stalk. Larger, lobed, toothed leaves occur in a cluster at the base of the plant. After the flowers fade, tiny black seeds sit exposed in the cup-like open capsule. Raindrops disperse the seeds by splashing them to the ground.

Bishop's-cap is typical of rich woods in the eastern United States. In the Great Lakes region, it occurs also in moister situations.

Goldenseal
Hydrastis canadensis
Buttercup Family

Goldenseal is an acclaimed medicinal herb used widely for years as a general tonic and in many locales is a vicitm of over-collection. Its creeping yellow rhizomes produce discrete colonies of perennial plants having single, unbranched stems; tough, prominently veined leaves that persist until fall; and solitary white flowers. Emerging stems are bent over but straighten revealing developing leaves and, in May, greenish-white, half-inch flowers consisting of a mass of white stamens. Short-lived, the flowers give way to inedible bright red berries by midsummer.

Found in rich woods from New England westward to Minnesota, Nebraska, and Arkansas and south into Alabama and Georgia, Goldenseal is now reappearing in some locations where it was once over-collected.

Blue-eyed Mary
Collinsia verna
Snapdragon Family

Although commonly known as Blue-eyed Mary, this spring-flowering species takes the name of its genus from English botanist Zaccheus Collins. Without flowers, it is recognizable by leaf bases that clasp the 1- to 2-foot stem and rows of tiny hairs arranged in a linear fashion along the length of the stem. In May or June, its blue and white flowers form tiers in typical groups of 5 or 6 around the weak, slender stalks.

Blue-eyed Mary inhabits rich woods from New York to the Midwest and south to Virginia and Tennessee where it also grows in woodland borders under less restricted light conditions. Though not considered rare throughout its range, Blue-eyed Mary will likely be encountered with less frequency in our region than farther south.

May-apple
Podophyllum peltatum
Barberry Family

A spreading plant that forms continually expanding colonies, May-apple prefers low, moist deciduous woods. The leaves of this 1- to 2-foot perennial are large, umbrella-shaped, and somewhat divided. From April to early June, a single, 2-inch creamy white flower may droop from the fork between paired leaves where it is inconspicuous to most observers but easily found by foraging bumblebees. After flowering, the plants produce egg-sized yellowish fruits considered by some to be edible at maturity. However, immature fruits as well as all other plant parts contain the poison podophyllin, so eating any part of this plant is best avoided.

May-apple is widely distributed from Quebec and Ontario to Florida and Texas.

fwc

Wild Blue Phlox
Phlox divaricata
Phlox Family

A characteristic wildflower of the spring woods, Wild Blue Phlox blooms between April and early June after the early spring flowers peak and just before the trees fully leaf out. Erect flowering stems up to 18 inches tall arise from partially reclining basal shoots that form loose clumps. The narrow, pointed upper leaves opposite each other on the slightly wooly stems contrast with the wider, ovate basal leaves.

A delightful pale to dark blue color, the fragrant flowers are tubular and 5-lobed as is typical of phlox flowers. They occur in clusters at the tips of the stems. Butterflies love this easily cultivated species.

Wild Blue Phlox flourishes in the rich soil of woodlands and flower gardens. It grows naturally in Vermont and parts of Quebec west to Illinois and south to Alabama and South Carolina.

fwc

Spiderwort
Tradescantia virginiana
Spiderwort Family

Cottony hair among the flowers and clustering of narrow leaves under the flowers in this species combine to suggest the common name Spiderwort. A tough perennial of moist woods and meadows, Spiderwort bears stems up to 12 inches tall with thin, dull green leaves of similar length. Flowers form at the ends of short stalks from spring to early summer, lasting individually only a day although plants will produce blooms for an entire month. Usually cyan-blue, the blossoms can also be purple, rose, or white in color.

Spiderwort grows in thickets and woods from Missouri to Georgia north into Maine, Connecticut, and Wisconsin.

Wild Geranium; Crane's-bill
Geranium maculatum
Geranium Family

Wild Geranium is one of the most common flowers of spring and one of the most satisfactory garden wildflowers. Hairy, erect, and bushy, this perennial grows from a fleshy rhizome, sending up solitary stems a foot or more tall with divided, toothed leaves, the basal ones often larger and on long stalks.

In May and June, 5-petaled flowers as large as 1½ inches across occur in clusters above the leaves. Ranging in color from pink (most common) to light purple and rarely white, each flower lasts only two days. On the first day, the stamens mature and the plant is functionally a male. The following day the male anthers fall off and the stigmas open, making the flower functionally female. This separation of the sexes by timing within a single flower ensures cross pollination by insects between flowers .

The dispersal mechanism of this plant is also worth noting. Each of the 5 fruit sections splits off from the others when dry, curls up on its stalk, twists as humidity changes, and expels itself to land some distance away.

Found in moist woods and thickets and along roadsides from Maine to Manitoba south and east to Missouri, Kansas, Georgia, and Tennessee, Wild Geranium can slowly spread forming small colonies.

Violets

One of the most familiar of wild-flowers, violets resemble pansies to which they are related. Their bilaterally symmetrical blossoms have 2 upper and 3 lower petals. The larger lowermost petal usually features a tubular spur, and the petals often display dark brown-purple lines that direct visiting insects. Within the many species of violets, two growth patterns exist. In the first, creeping, branching stems are entirely underground. Individual leaves and flowers arise from this underground stem. The second form features leaves and flowers produced on branched, erect, zigzagged stems that grow above ground. Most violets, including all shown here, produce inconspicuous, self-fertilizing (cleistogamous) flowers underground later in the season. These flowers lack petals and never open but generate copious seeds.

The 4 violets illustrated here are but a few of the numerous species found in this region, many of which hybridize making identification difficult.

Common Blue Violet; Woolly Blue Violet
Viola sororia
Violet Family

The only violet included herein that produces its leaves and flowers from undergound stems, this wide-ranging species has heart-shaped leaves. Lower leaf surfaces and stems are woolly. The showy blue flowers appear from March to early June on hairy stalks that often exceed the leaves in height. One of many native and introduced blue violets, Common Blue Violet ranges from Quebec to South Dakota south to Oklahoma, Missouri, Kentucky, and North Carolina. It inhabits low moist forests and clearings.

Long-spurred Violet
Viola rostrata
Violet Family

A spur that projects some distance up and back from the flower distinguishes Long-spurred Violet from its blue-flowered relatives. Somewhat small and tending to form discrete clumps of closely crowded above-ground stems, it puts on height after blooming. This often pale or steely blue violet with a pronounced dark eye at its center blooms from April to June. It typically occupies calcareous woods from Quebec to Wisconsin and in much of southern New England south to Georgia and Alabama.

Yellow Violet
Viola pubescens
Violet Family

Yellow flowers with purple veins make this perennial very recognizable in May and early June. At other times its "downy" leaves and stems are an aid to identification. The only wide-spread yellow violet native to our area, it can be 4 to 12 inches tall with 1 to few leafy above-ground stems. Ranging from southern Quebec, Maine, and South Dakota south to Tennessee and west to Missouri and Nebraska, it inhabits rich woods, often in fairly large patches, and may bloom again in the fall.

Canada Violet
Viola canadensis
Violet Family

White with purple veining and often blue on the back side of the petals, Canada Violet blooms on erect stems from late April through July and occasionally to October. Numerous leaves occur widely spaced below and crowded near the top of the above-ground stem. Like many other plants, it bears the species name *canadensis* denoting the location of its original discovery. Found mainly in upland forests, Canada Violet grows from Quebec and New Hampshire south to South Carolina and Alabama and west to Montana and South Dakota.

Foamflower; False Miterwort
Tiarella cordifolia
Saxifrage Family

Tiny fly-pollinated white flowers forming a loose cylinder around a narrow erect stalk mark this dainty wildflower. Rarely more than 1 foot tall, Foamflower features basal semi-evergreen leaves shaped somewhat like maple leaves and sometimes marked with red blotches or a network of lines. Each single plant may form many runners and thus in time produce numerous flowering individuals that often create an extensive ground cover in the woods. The larger the population, the more spectacular is the effect of mounds of foam when it blooms in May and June.

Foamflower grows throughout the southern and eastern United States north to Ontario and Nova Scotia. Frequent in the eastern portion of our region, Foamflower barely enters Wisconsin except within a few miles of the Lake Michigan shoreline.

Wild Leek; Ramps
Allium tricoccum
Lily Family

Many people value Wild Leek as a food flavoring. But those who regularly eat its onion-scented bulb will have difficulty in hiding their dietary choice as the pungent flavor produces strong breath and body odor.

Found throughout most of the eastern United States and adjacent Canada, Wild Leek often grows in large clumps from clustered bulbs. The plants produce 8- to 12-inch-long broad, fleshy, pointed elliptic leaves that disappear in late spring or early summer. Later, spherical clusters of white flowers top 1-foot stalks. After flowering, each round generally fleshy fruit dries out and splits open releasing shiny black seeds. The species name *tricoccum*, meaning 3 round parts, refers to the 3 chambers in this dry capsule.

Broad-leaved Waterleaf; Canada Waterleaf
Hydrophyllum canadense
Waterleaf Family

Broad-leaved Waterleaf grows 8 to 18 inches tall with thin, slightly roughened leaves having 5 to 7 lobes that radiate out like fingers, maple-like. The leaves appear early and are considered by some a choice, edible spring herb. Miniature basal leaves may be somewhat evergreen in milder climates.

An erect, smooth perennial, Broad-leaved Waterleaf flowers in June and July with clusters of lavender blue to pale purple blossoms 1 inch across or less and not very distinctive. Found throughout the eastern United States and into southern Ontario, it can become quite prolific in the wildflower garden.

Virginia Waterleaf
Hydrophyllum virginianum
Waterleaf Family

The common and family name of waterleaf species refers to the succulent nature of the stems and leaves – not to their typical habitats in moist, rich woods. The leaves of Virginia Waterleaf have lobes scattered along both sides of a central axis and frequently exhibit white blotches resembling watermarks. Pale lavender to white flowers in a somewhat spherical cluster appear among the leaves on erect, smooth stems up to 1 foot tall in late spring.

Virginia Waterleaf ranges from Manitoba and southern Ontario to Massachusetts and Vermont south to Alabama, Arkansas, Kansas, and Missouri.

Dwarf Ginseng
Panax trifolius
Ginseng Family

More delicate than its sister species Ginseng, Dwarf Ginseng is a miniature plant usually no more than 6 to 8 inches tall. Often occurring in small dense patches, each plant arises from a pea-sized round tuber several inches underground. This smooth perennial produces several leaves having 3 leaflets each and spherical clusters of tiny white flowers between April and June. Unlike its larger cousin, its root has no reputed medicinal value.

Dwarf Ginseng ranges widely from Prince Edward Island to Minnesota and south as far as north Georgia.

Ginseng; "Sang"
Panax quinquefolius
Ginseng Family

Widely valued for the alleged therapeutic or aphrodisiac value of its large root, particularly in China, Ginseng has been a target of collectors since Colonial times. Daniel Boone reputedly earned part of his living collecting Ginseng for trade. Its range extends throughout eastern North America, but it is now rare across much of that range as a result of over-collecting.

Ginseng is a perennial up to 1 foot tall with compound leaves typically consisting of 5 long, pointed lobes. Even when tiny umbels of white flowers appear in June and July, the leaves, similar to those of many other woodland species, render the plants inconspicuous. Pollinated by flies, the flower cluster arises from the center of the leaves, followed in the fall by red, fleshy berries that bear seeds requiring 2 to several years to germinate.

False Spikenard
Smilacina racemosa
Lily Family

False Spikenard is renowned both for its flowers and its fruit. Its unbranched, hairy stems arise from underground rhizomes and arch gracefully. Reaching heights of 16 to 36 inches, each has as many as 12 to 25 or more oval-shaped leaves arranged along the stem in ranks as if to take maximum advantage of sunlight. Flowering occurs from May to July when a terminal, branched, cone-shaped cluster (panicle) of tiny creamy-white flowers appears. Each flower gives rise to a berry in the fall that is first pink and then red. A preferred food source of birds, the berries form as early as July and typically remain on the plant through September.

Widely distributed in Canada from British Columbia to Quebec and Nova Scotia, False Spikenard occurs in the United States from New England west to Tennessee and Missouri. It is quite common in the southern Great Lakes region.

American Columbo
Frasera caroliniensis
Gentian Family

A giant among herbaceous plants, often 6 to 8 feet tall, American Columbo is monocarpic meaning it flowers once and dies. The plant first forms a rosette of large basal leaves, often up to 2 feet long, from a large underground root. This rosette may grow for several years until the plant accumulates sufficient food to bloom. The following spring it will send up a giant flowering stalk with many flowers, set seed, and die.

The leaves of the flowering stalk occur in whorls, several from one node. Darkly spotted greenish-yellow flowers about 1-inch across top the leaf whorls in late spring. Conspicuous on the petals are hairy, fringed, circular nectar glands that are attractive to insects.

Found from Ontario down through the Midwest and the southern Appalachians, American Columbo grows in rich woods, on somewhat dry meadows, and along roadsides. Colonies often contain a few flowering plants and numerous non-flowering ones.

Lousewort
Pedicularis canadensis
Snapdragon Family

This unusual member of the Snapdragon Family is said to be partly parasitic on the roots of grasses or other woodland plants. Growing up to a foot tall, the perennial plants are coarse and densely hairy with long, sharply divided basal leaves and clustered stems. From April to June, loose flower heads at the ends of dense, leafy, terminal spikes bear ³/₄-inch flowers varying from creamy yellow to reddish purple in color. Occasional plants appear to lack green color and may be dark purple.

Difficult if not impossible to transplant, Lousewort is widely distributed in eastern and central North America.

Swamp Buttercup
Ranunculus hispidus
Buttercup Family

As its common name clearly denotes, this species of buttercup prefers moist woods and swampy habitats. A slender, tufted perennial, Swamp Buttercup has deeply parted leaves with 3 to 5 wedge-shaped segments per leaf. Its flowers appear from March to June with waxy, bright yellow petals typical of buttercups and last only a few days. Clusters of dry seeds follow the flowers.

Swamp Buttercup grows across the South from Arkansas to Georgia and from Missouri into Michigan, Ohio, and New York in the northern United States.

42

taf

Wild Columbine
Aquilegia canadensis
Buttercup Family

Widely cultivated and variable, Wild Columbine is a graceful, many-branched perennial and a popular choice for wildflower gardens. Leaf size, flower color, and plant size can differ widely, the latter from 8 inches to 3 feet depending on growing conditions. From April to mid-May, solitary scarlet and yellow flowers nod at the tips of the slender branches. Each flower displays 5 petals, each petal with a long spur. Capable of reaching the nectar at the base of these spurs, Hummingbirds are frequent visitors during its flowering period.

Although typical of deciduous woods and clearings, Wild Columbine also grows in such places as rocky outcrops, meadows, and shores. Its wide area of distribution includes eastern and southern Canada as well as the eastern and midwestern United States.

fwc

Red Baneberry
Actaea rubra
Buttercup Family

White Baneberry; Doll's-eyes
Actaea pachypoda
Buttercup Family

Baneberry plants are commonly 18 to 24 inches tall with compound leaves of many leaflets, those of Red Baneberry having minute hairs on the underside. Borne below the flowering scape, the leaves are fully formed by the time flowers appear.

Rounded or elongated clusters of tiny white flowers bloom in May or June in both species of baneberry. Red Baneberry produces compact clusters of fruits on thin, wiry stalks, the bright red fruits maturing in mid-summer. Reaching maturity slightly later, the white, porcelain-like, somewhat fleshy fruits of White Baneberry occur in elongate clusters. Widely spaced on thick reddish stalks, each White Baneberry fruit features a single dark "eye spot" or "Doll's-eye," the latter being an alternate common name for that species. Fruits of both species are poisonous if ingested, giving rise to their shared common name "bane"-berry.

Red Baneberry ranges from Labrador across to British Columbia south to New Jersey, West Virginia, Ohio, Indiana, Iowa, Colorado, Utah, and Oregon in a variety of deciduous and coniferous forests. White Baneberry is common in most of the eastern United States and occurs from Nova Scotia to Manitoba in Canada south to Georgia, Alabama, and Oklahoma.

fwc

Partridge-berry
Mitchella repens
Madder Family

Exhibiting small evergreen leaves, this ground cover grows in sterile, acid, sandy soil in almost any kind of forest cover, especially wherever it is not subject to heavy leaf litter. Its half-inch oval leaves are paired along creeping stems that climb over rocks, logs, and moss. In late June and July, paired small white flowers, united at their bases, present a striking contrast to the dark green of the leaves. The 4-pointed petals of the flowers open revealing the reproductive parts. Cross pollination results in bright red berries, each the product of 2 flowers and therefore bearing 2 scars. Unless eaten by birds, the berries persist on the plant throughout winter.

Designated by at least 25 common names, Partridge-berry ranges from Newfoundland to Ontario and Minnesota south to Texas and Florida in a variety of habitats.

Strawberry Blite
Chenopodium capitatum
Goosefoot Family

Strawberry Blite is an annual that prefers recently disturbed situations, i.e. new roadside gradings, dumps, and gravel pits in wooded areas. Appearing within 1 to 2 years after disturbance, the plant can persist 2 to 3 years at a site then disappears as competition develops. It reaches heights of 2 feet or taller but often tends to fall over from the weight of its strawberry-like fruits that follow the masses of inconspicuous small flowers. With its extended blooming period from June to August, Strawberry Blite can show bright red fruiting heads all summer.

The extensive range for this Eurasian species includes the midwestern and New England states as well as Alaska to Quebec and New Brunswick.

Wild Red Raspberry
Rubus strigosus
Rose Family

Closely allied to the raspberry clones of supermarket produce counters, this wild beauty produces scarlet, thimble-shaped (hollow) fruits in summer that are just as edible and tasty. The plants can grow 2 or more feet tall with leaves of 3 to 7 leaflets borne on upright stems. Less prickly than many of the other "brambles," it bears inconspicuous white flowers in early summer. Fruits follow on second-year canes, and the canes usually die after fruiting.

Wild Red Raspberry ranges worldwide in the north.

Squaw-root
Conopholis americana
Broom-rape Family

Easily recognized by its lack of any green color, Squaw-root is creamy white and occurs as a fleshy root parasite on oak in drier forests. Its rarely branched stems have brown-tipped, scale-like leaves arranged like a pinecone. They tend to push up through leaf litter in clumps to heights of 1 foot, though 6 inches is more typical. By flowering time between April and June, the scales become dry and hard, subtending the half-inch pale yellow, two-lipped flowers. Pollinated by insects, the flowers form rounded seed pods about the size of a small grape. The pods ripen in summer after which the clumps of stems turn brown and decompose.

Squaw-root occurs from Nova Scotia westward to the western Great Lakes region and south to Alabama and Florida.

taf

Indian-pipe
Monotropa uniflora
Indian-pipe Family

Indian-pipe is another species of plant devoid of chlorophyll. Mature stems of this species grow 6 to 8 inches tall. Waxy white in color, they recurve initially, so the individual flowers hang down like bells. Following pollination, the stems become stiffly erect and slowly dry out.

Young flowering stems emerge from under the leaves, their fragrance attracting pollinating bumblebees. The dust-like seeds from the drying plants are wind-dispersed. Soon after, the plants turn black and die.

Botanists once thought Indian-pipe to be a saprophyte utilizing dead plant material in the soil for food. They now believe, however, that it is an indirect parasite on nearby woody plants, obtaining food from a connecting (slave) fungus.

Of extremely wide distribution, Indian-pipe occurs in almost any kind of forest or thicket habitat including peat bogs and old fields throughout much of the United States, Canada, Mexico, and Asia.

Great Lakes Shorelines and Dunes

Our Great Lakes shorelines and dunes are not a specific habitat in the usual sense of having one fairly uniform set of conditions, as, for example, in sphagnum bog, old field, or deciduous forest. Rather, the combination of wave, ice, and wind action; fluctuating lake levels; temperature modification in winter; and cooling in summer produces a unique set of conditions of regular disturbance that arrest the usual process of plant succession. This disturbance allows the development of many colonies of plants that require open, competition-free soils to become established and to flourish in exceptional numbers. While only a few species are confined to these shoreline conditions alone, it is in this habitat that the most magnificent colonies and combinations of plants develop.

Being at one point flat sand beach; at another rolling dune and slack, in some places stabilized with developing cedar or pine forests; in another disturbed with blowing sand or moving dunes and in other instances wet soil or shallow pool, our shores present

many varied and subtle opportunities for plant community development. The common thread for all is open, raw soil. In some cases (low shorelines, dune slacks), water is readily available and in others (dune slopes and tops) there is very dry shifting sand.

Along the southern Great Lakes, temperatures climb high on the dunes in summer; in the north, temperatures tend to be moderated by the presence of the cold waters. Consequently, in southern lakeshore districts, some of the unusual plants coming from more southern or eastern Atlantic coastal plain districts establish and persist. On northern shorelines may be found plants predominantly of boreal affinity. When soils of limestone origin are present, species diversity tends to increase greatly. This is particularly true where the shoreline is relatively low and flat in limestone districts and there develops a mix of limy mud-flats, marl beds, shallow-watered fens, wet sands, and wooded low dune ridges that produces fantastic assemblages of wildflowers.

"The soil chemistry (pH) on the flats and in the sloughs is neutral or alkaline, . . . the vegetation fen-like. On the low dunes and ridges, drier conditions, quartz sands, and abundant conifer needle duff create a surface soil that is acid to subacid and support appropriately adapted plants" (Case, 1987, *Orchids of the Western Great Lakes Region*). Such conditions permit widely different levels of soil pH in close proximity. Because many of the species growing here are apparently indifferent to the amount of water present, provided their requirements of pH, humus, temperature, and competition are met, many of them can be found both on the wet marly flats and into the sandy ridges. Although appearing to be two different conditions, each situation falls within the range of tolerance for those species.

Our shorelines are home to striking assemblages and abundant mixtures of both plant individuals and species usually thought to be rare, local, or occupying a very narrow niche. Around pool edges and on bare mud flats grow

52

scattered clumps of pitcher-plants; butterworts (northern districts only); stunted plants of Yellow Lady's-slippers; sundews; and Bird's-eye Primroses, to be followed later in the season by Sticky Tofieldia, Rose Pogonia and Grass Pink orchids. Silver Cinquefoil spreads its runners in wet, stony sands. In limestone districts along the northern rim of Lakes Huron and Michigan, low moist gravels, wet sands, and especially lightly shaded edges of developing cedar woods may be carpeted with Dwarf Lake Iris interlaced with massive flowering colonies of Fringed Polygala. In somewhat drier marly muds, Shrubby Cinquefoil dominates with its brilliant yellow summer flowers. In moist shade of low ridges and dune slopes, Labrador-tea, Leatherleaf, and northern honeysuckles may dominate.

On ridges and low dunes, various dune grasses, sage, Bearberry, and trailing as well as spreading junipers are first to develop, followed in northern districts by white cedars, spruces, and firs and on drier sites by Jack Pine

and Red (*Pinus resinosa*) and White Pines. On the higher grounds, the wildflower flora is much the same as that of our Jack Pine and other pine woodlands away from the dunes: Starflower, Bunchberry, Twinflower, Sweet White Violets, Ram's-head and Pink Lady's-slippers, and, in coldest districts, Calypso orchids. Open sandy dunes support Puccoon and even Morel Mushrooms.

Mid-summer finds vast displays of Pearly Everlasting, Pitcher's Thistle, acres of yellow Coreopsis, and the delicate beauty of Bluebell in moist to dry sands. Wet sloughs glow yellow with the snapdragon-like flowers of carnivorous bladderworts. Fall brings the green-white White Camas and the yellow of goldenrods, some of them endangered.

The delicate, dazzling beauty of this assemblage of natural communities is among the most threatened of our wildflower habitats. Greatest danger and damage come from real estate development with cottage lawns and buildings replacing the native species.

Even more damaging today are the massive conglomerate condominiums consuming available lakeshore in many places. Off road recreation vehicles form ruts in the mud and do incalculable damage to plant and animal habitats. While the species here thrive on gradual disturbance, they cannot cope with the rapid changes wrought by wheeled vehicles and buildings. Because these marl flat, dune, and slack habitats are unique assemblages found only along the freshwater Great Lakes and because their beauty is great, their destruction is inexcusable.

Conservation groups, public authorities, and local governments need to do more to protect and preserve this spectacular and endangered habitat in its pristine, natural state.

fwc

Fringed Polygala
Polygala paucifolia
Milkwort Family

A tiny plant scarcely 4 inches tall, Fringed Polygala often occurs in dense colonies in a variety of habitats throughout the northern Great Lakes. Preferring sandy, humus-rich soil, it produces predominantly rose-purple flowers in May or June in our region. White and pale pink forms also occur. One of the petals of the 1-inch flowers is keel-shaped and crested on the back. Two side petals resemble wings, giving rise to the common name Gaywings. Its common name Flowering Wintergreen refers to the resemblence of its leaves, not its flowers, to Wintergreen. Throughout the summer and fall, these plants produce tiny, non-opening, self-fertilizing (cleistogamous) flowers on underground branches.

Fringed Polygala grows as far north as the Gaspé Peninsula and Quebec to Manitoba, south into New England and the Lakes States and very locally into the southern mountains.

Calypso; Fairy's-slipper
Calypso bulbosa
Orchid Family

One of two Calypso forms occurring in North America, our form ranges throughout the northern continent from the east coast to Alaska and is locally abundant in coniferous forests of the Rockies into Arizona and New Mexico. Requiring cool soil at its corm and having flower buds extremely sensitive to frost, it occupies only habitats where snow persists until after the last frost or retards growth until all danger of frost is past.

Calypso belongs to a peculiar orchid group that produces its leaf in late October. The leaf lasts through winter, withering shortly after flowering occurs. Blooming between May and July on plants only 4 to 7 inches tall, the delicate 1- to 1½-inch flowers have outward-folding lip margins that form an apron outside the lip, unlike the lip margins of the lady's-slippers that fold inward. (See also in Northern Coniferous Forests)

fwc

Ram's-head Lady's-Slipper
Cypripedium arietinum
Orchid Family

The Ram's-head Lady's-slippers are small and so inconspicuous that they are usually overlooked, even when flowering in late May or June. The 5- to 12-inch stems bear 1-inch pouches of reddish- or brownish-purple and white with hairs that give them a frosted appearance. The separated lower sepals distinguish this primitive slipper from most other slippers which have those sepals united. Its common name derives from the elongation of the lower front of the pouch to resemble a ram's snout. This lady's-slipper usually has 3 to 4 bluish green leaves whose attachment points spiral around the stem instead of being arranged in ranks one above the other as in the Yellow Lady's-slipper.

Although this species is generally rare, large populations of Ram's-head Lady's-slippers exist locally in cool dune woods of Canada Balsam, Jack Pine, and White Cedar in the upper Great Lakes region of Ontario and Michigan. In Wisconsin, Minnesota, and northwestern Lake Superior, it is very rare and local.

fwc

fwc

fwc

Dwarf Lake Iris
Iris lacustris
Iris Family

Only the western Great Lakes region can claim this small beauty among its native flora. A signature plant of northern Lakes Huron and Michigan, Dwarf Lake Iris presently grows principally along the shorelines of upper Lakes Huron and Michigan and is a federally threatened species. Due to habitat destruction, primarily for recreational and residential development, it is now extinct in its former southern disjunct occurrences in the region. Despite this restricted range, local ground-carpeting colonies exist near the Great Lakes shores only, in strictly limestone districts. Some of the densest colonies occur in Door County, Wisconsin.

One of the smallest of all irises, this dwarf species produces typically blue-purple flowers in May and June. Blossoms 2 inches across top 3- to 4-inch stems that emerge amid the 3- to 5-inch fan of leaves before they reach full size. White mutants occur occasionally.

Blue-eyed Grass

Sisyrinchium angustifolium
Iris Family

The narrow, grass-like leaves of this iris relative can be up to a foot long. Winged flower stems produce a 2-leaved spathe from which emerge upright or dangling flowers in late spring to early summer. Blue to violet in color, the petals of the half-inch blossoms are linear to ovate in shape. Round, reddish-brown seed capsules, usually dangling, follow the flowers in late summer.

Blue-eyed Grass occurs as scattered plants or in large colonies. A plant of damp shores, meadows, and thickets, it can be found from Florida to east Texas north to southeast Newfoundland, southern Quebec, southern Ontario, Ohio, Indiana, Illinois, Missouri, and eastern Kansas.

Bird's-eye Primrose

Primula mistassinica
Primrose Family

Bird's-eye Primrose, our only native primrose, possesses tiny 2-inch rosettes of toothed leaves, yellowish green above with silver-white meal beneath. From the rosette arises a disproportionately large stem up to 6 inches tall that produces loosely rounded heads of 3 to 6 flowers. The notched lavender petals are yellow at their bases where they unite in a tubular arrangement. Their top portion flares out trumpet-like from the tube revealing the characteristic yellow "bird's-eye" center of the flowers. Also distinctive is their sweet, pungent aroma.

Bird's-eye Primrose usually occurs in dense stands of many plants on dripping calcareous ledges, in marl fens, on wet sands of interdunal swales and shorelines, and sometimes on lawns. It ranges from coast to coast in the far north of North America and south in the Great Lakes region to a few inland fens in southern Michigan.

Butterwort
Pinguicula vulgaris
Bladderwort Family

This carnivorous butterwort, a plant of marl fens, calcareous sands, and moist, calcareous rock faces, occurs throughout northern North America. It is always in wet habitats and almost always near the Great Lakes shores. Exceptions occur in inland fens near St. Ignace and on limestone river cliffs in southwest Ontario.

The plants feature 2- to 4-inch basal rosettes of saucer-like leaves, yellow-green with upfolded margins. Like other carnivorous plants, Butterwort grows in habitats where nutrients are limited. Glands on the leaf surface produce digestive secretions, described as "buttery," that trap insects, primarily gnats and flies, and digest them. In late June and July, striking purple flowers somewhat like violets appear on flowering stems up to 6 inches tall. Laplanders use Butterwort leaves to curdle reindeer milk, producing their version of cottage cheese.

Sticky Tofieldia; False Asphodel
Tofieldia glutinosa
Lily Family

Sticky hairs covering the stems and the leaves of this plant make it very easy to identify. With leaves occurring in 2- to 5-inch tufts reminiscent of small iris plants, Sticky Tofieldia grows almost exclusively in damp, limy sites along rocky shorelines and in marshes and fens, frequently with Grass-of-Parnassus. From June to August, flower spikes up to 1 foot tall display dense heads of starry white flowers. Individual flowers are minute, but the heads can be quite showy. Dry seed capsules rather than berries follow the flowers.

Broom-rape; Cancer-root
Orobanche uniflora
Broom-rape Family

Broom-rape is one of a relatively few flowering plant species that lack chlorophyll. Found primarily on dunes in the Great Lakes, it can also occur on oak savannas and prairies and in dry cedar woods. It ranges from New Brunswick to Montana and south to Florida, Mississippi, and Texas.

The creamy colored plants with a hint of gray or silver-blue often grow in clumps of many stems up to 6 inches tall. In May and June, each stem produces a single tubular flower creamy white to lilac in color and having two yellow ridges in the throat.

Broom-rape is reported to parasitize various plants, but documentation for its attachment exists only for asters and goldenrods in Michigan (Voss, 1996).

Red Anemone
Anemone multifida
Buttercup Family

Red Anemone is an early summer flowering perennial that grows from a tight rootstock particularly adapted to holding moisture. Ranging across the continent in cool climates from Newfoundland to Alaska, it avoids competition with other plants, occurring typically in shifting sands, on rocky ledges, and in gravely spots. In our region it is confined to sandy habitats, usually dunes and shores, and rarely further inland in Jack Pine plains.

Plants 6 to 9 inches tall produce much-divided leaves from a stout stem. Borne singly on stems arising from the crown, flowers can be up to 1 inch wide in a variety of colors – white, cream, yellow, pink, and red – with reds predominating in this region. Like many members of its family, Red Anemone has only sepals, which serve the same function as petals – namely insect attraction.

59

Indian Paintbrush
Castilleja coccinea
Snapdragon Family

One of the spectacular sights of dune slacks, interdunal flats, and low roadsides in the northern Great Lakes region is the brilliant scarlet display of Indian Paintbrush. The showiest aspect of this wide-ranging species, as in the Poinsettia, is its colorful modified leaves or bracts rather than flower parts. The actual greenish flowers occur from May to July in the angles between the stem and the bract and are somewhat tubular in shape. Only the flower tips are as brightly colored as the bracts.

Indian Paintbrush can be up to 2 feet tall and features a hairy stem. Despite green leaves that carry out photosynthesis, in its first year it is a hemiparasite, attaching some of its roots to nearby grasses and other herbaceous plants. For this reason it is difficult to cultivate at this stage, but plants transplanted early in the second year may continue to grow, develop, and flower.

Native from New Hampshire to Manitoba south to Florida and Oklahoma, it ranges throughout our region but is most often seen in the north.

Bearberry
Arctostaphylos uva-ursi
Heath Family

Bearberry is difficult to establish in cultivation but ironically grows in some of the harshest sandy soil of the Great Lakes region. Found abundantly on dunes and throughout Jack Pine plains as well as on rocky ledges and outcrops in bright sun, it ranges from Alaska to Newfoundland south to the Great Lakes dunes and throughout the western Rockies as well as across Europe and Asia. Nurseries in our area frequently offer propogated specimens to gardeners as a groundcover.

A low, trailing shrub with stems typically running along the ground, Bearberry features hard, leathery, glossy, evergreen leaves that persist for several years. Clusters of pink to white flowers occur in spring followed by large, showy but dryish and insipid red berries that last into winter providing food for birds and other wildlife.

False Solomon-seal
Smilacina stellata
Lily Family

The extensive underground stems of this species enable single plants to form dense colonies along the Great Lakes shores and in nearby thickets. Particularly abundant on dunes and beaches, False Solomon-seal occurs in inland meadows as well. Its upright, or sometimes arching, slightly zigzagged stems feature leaves in two ranks along each side and can vary in size from 6 inches to 2 feet in height. Beginning in May and extending into early summer, 10 to 30 small, showy white flowers emerge on long, stiffly erect pedicels. Following the flowers are berries that become reddish-brown with purplish-black markings.

False Solomon-seal occurs from Newfoundland to British Columbia south to California, upland Arizona, New Mexico, and Kansas across to West Virginia and Pennsylvania.

Sand Coreopsis; Long-stalk Tickseed
Coreopsis lanceolata
Aster or Daisy Family

Sand Coreopsis grows best in rocky or sandy soil in the wild, occurring in this region on sand dunes and shores, in Jack Pine clearings, and on limestone pavements and gravel on the Bruce Peninsula and Manitoulin Island. Able to form dense colonies, it is particularly abundant in the vicinity of the Straits of Mackinac. It also thrives under cultivation and is widespread as a garden escape.

The leaves of Sand Coreopsis usually have smaller lobes near their base and somewhat elongated runners arising from the base of the plant, making it very recognizable. Bright yellow flowers 2 to 3 inches in diameter appear from May to July on the short-lived, sun-loving plants.

Silverweed
Potentilla anserina
Rose Family

Silverweed is so named because long silky hairs on the lower leaf surfaces give them a silver color. A typical shoreline plant of low, moist sands and gravel and interdunal swales in the Great Lakes region, Silverweed typically grows to a height of 4 to 5 inches. In stable situations, it can occur in large dense colonies formed by runners from the often reddish-colored above-ground stems. Brilliant yellow flowers up to 1 inch in diameter provide a showy presence from June to August even though they are only 1 to 2 inches above ground.

The plant ranges from Newfoundland to Alaska south to New York, Indiana, and Iowa.

Sand Heather; Beach-heath; False Heather
Hudsonia tomentosa
Rockrose Family

Sand Heather is characteristic of sand blows on shifting dunes and shorelines and is almost never found inland in our region. Usually appearing as scattered clumps or tufts up to a foot across but only 3 to 4 inches tall, the plants have scale-like or needle-like leaves closely overlapped and covered with hairs. The leaves give the plants a gray cast and make them resemble somewhat the Trailing Juniper. In June and July, they produce abundant tiny, yellow, starry flowers.

Native from Quebec to Alberta south to southwest Ontario, Indiana, and Minnesota, Sand Heather ranges as far south as North Carolina in the southern Appalachians where it grows on rocky outcrops and may reach heights up to 1 foot.

Hairy Puccoon
Lithospermum caroliniense
Borage Family

Among yellow-flowered dune species, this one stands out for the richness of its orange-yellow color. From late May through June, its flowers open a few at a time from the top of a continuously uncoiling inflorescence with petals united into a trumpet-like tube.

Hairy Puccoon occurs in several varieties and ranges from the upper Great Lakes south to Florida, Texas, and Mexico. Found on dunes and in sandy Jack Pine woods, the Great Lakes variety reaches heights of 12 to 18 inches. It sometimes occurs in more or less erect multi-stemmed clumps, and its narrow leaves are covered with fine hairs.

65

Harebell; Bluebell
Campanula rotundifolia
Bluebell Family

The Latin name for this species means "round-leaved little bell." Its basal leaves are somewhat round but often not seen since they tend to wither by the mid-summer flowering time. Stem leaves, by contrast, are linear.

Variable in size and shape, Harebells most typically grow to 12 to 18 inches tall with flowers frequently a distinctive delicate blue. White and dwarf forms, though, do occur. Frequently grown in cultivation, they are particularly abundant on Great Lakes dunes but also occur inland in sandy habitats as well.

Occurring across North America in the north, Harebells extend southward along the mountains and shorelines of California back through New Mexico and Arizona to West Virginia.

Beach Pea
Lathyrus japonicus
Pea Family

The compound leaves of this widely distributed and highly variable perennial are interesting in that several of the terminal leaflets are modified into tendrils that wrap around nearby vegetation providing support for this weak plant. Found worldwide in the northern hemisphere on beaches and shores, both fresh and salt water, Beach Pea produces 1-inch blue-violet "sweet pea" flowers from June to September.

Kalm's St. John's-wort
Hypericum kalmianum
St. John's-wort Family

Named in honor of Peter Kalm, an early explorer, this species usually grows on the wetter parts of dunes and on lake plain prairies. Its semi-woody stems grow to 2 feet tall and appear angular or square in cross-section. Leaves are dark green and narrow with distinctive tiny black dots on their undersides. July and August bring 1-inch flowers with bright yellow stems, reflexed petals, and clusters of conspicuous stamens.

Lake Huron Tansy
Tanacetum huronense
Aster or Daisy Family

Lake Huron Tansy, first described by early botanist Thomas Nuttall from the Straits of Mackinac, is very local in the Great Lakes region and now on the threatened list of plants for the state of Michigan. Ranging across the continent in the north, it favors calcareous sands along the Great Lakes shoreline in this region. Plants occur as scattered stems that grow up to 18 inches tall with finely divided hairy leaves reminiscent of ferns and distinctive for their medicinal aroma. From June to August, 1-inch yellow button-like heads of disk flowers appear, the ray flowers typical of this family lacking or much reduced.

Pitcher's Thistle; Dune Thistle
Cirsium pitcheri
Aster or Daisy Family

Once found on dunes all around Lakes Michigan and Huron, Pitcher's Thistle is now quite rare or extinct in the southern portion of that range due to development and/or habitat disturbance. On Lake Superior, where it was originally found in 1829, only one location is known for this species.

Pitcher's Thistle is monocarpic, flowering only once after several years of growth before dying. Achieving heights up to 3 to 4 feet, the plant accumulates food until it has sufficient nourishment to produce creamy-white flowers. For the first year or more, only a basal cluster of spiny, silver-gray, deeply lobed leaves may be in evidence. The white coating reflects much incidental light (heat) that falls on the young plant.

White Camas; Death Camas
Zigadenus glaucus
Lily Family

Narrow, leathery, silver-green keeled leaves clustered at the base of the stem characterize this plant of dunes and other Great Lakes sandy or rocky shores. Sometimes also found inland, White Camas contains an alkaloid, particularly in the bulb, that is poisonous to humans and other animals. A spike arising from the tuft of basal leaves produces a raceme of somewhat flat, cupped, bi-colored flowers that appear whitish-green. Close examination of the flowers will reveal both a strong, unpleasant odor and glistening greenish nectar glands. Flowering occurs from mid-July to September.

White Camas occurs on calcareous soils from Quebec to Minnesota south to New England, Ohio, and Illinois.

Beach Grass
Ammophila breviligulata
Grass Family

A single "plant" of this species may occupy extensive areas of a dune. Its underground creeping stems effectively colonize and stabilize the shifting sands, sending up leafy shoots to 3 feet tall and, in mid- to late summer, flowering stems to 5 feet tall with dense, spike-like clusters of small wind-pollinated flowers. The bluish-gray color of the leaves is distinctive and indicates a waxy coating that may help resist drying.

Wherever it occurs, from Newfoundland and Labrador to the Great Lakes shores south to Pennsylvania and North Carolina, Beach Grass is most important as a dune building agent. It is able to maintain growth as sand accumulates and buries its stem base.

Dune Grass
Elymus mollis
Grass Family

Frequently sharing sands with Beach Grass, Dune Grass forms large clumps of plants up to 3 feet tall with robust leaves almost 1 inch wide. The bent, blowing leaves may produce interesting concentric markings in the sand as seen in the photograph. Sturdy flowering stalks terminate in "wheatlike" flowers in June and July. Like other beach grasses, it binds the sands and slows their movement, paving the way for greater stabilization.

A widespread species along shorelines across northern North America, Dune Grass grows almost exclusively on the beaches and dunes of Lake Superior in the Great Lakes region where it is rare. This handsome grass is especially well developed at Michigan's Whitefish Point.

Streambanks and Floodplain Forests

Many plants have fairly wide habitat tolerances, providing their key requirements are met. For most plants of streambanks and floodplain forests, the critical factors are soil moisture, suitable light levels, and a proper acidity or alkalinity (pH) range. If these factors are within the plant's tolerances, it will grow there.

Conditions on streambanks may be quite varied. The typical smaller midwestern stream drains a geologically less mature region with more heterogeneous upland soils than occur on the larger river floodplain. Being less subject to flooding than the larger river the stream feeds, the streambanks here may contain only small areas of allu-

vial deposit. Acid soils may occur just a few feet away from a calcareous seepage slope. Soils may be coarse, fine, or of mixed texture, each condition providing a different degree of drainage and oxygen content. Springs, seepage slopes, and mucky thickets may alternate with well-drained upland vegetation right to the water's edge. Conditions of natural disturbance, erosion, downed trees, or beaver activity may create temporary or relatively permanent open, sunny, marsh-like conditions. Since there is no common thread to this mosaic of plant communities except moisture, light, and pH, few streambank wildflowers grow exclusively there. Rather they occur in a

wide variety of habitats. Those we illustrate here are the showier species one can often locate easily by exploring along a brook or streambank.

River floodplains are less varied. By definition a characteristic feature of old age and mature river development, the river floodplain is a large area of relatively flat, poorly drained deposits laid down as the river meanders from side to side. Because such soils were carried in suspension and deposited by settling from the floodwaters, they tend to be of a relatively uniform silt or clay. Sandier or more gravely levee, laid down when fast-moving floodwaters slow as the flood recedes, may intersperse with the silt or clay, particularly

near the riverbank. Floodplains are subject to frequent flooding from snowbank and run-off waters. Periodically larger floods may occur in any season. Frequently the soil pH is neutral or alkaline, the soil quite fertile, and since the land is low, the water table high year round.

If a floodplain is open, marsh vegetation may prevail. If wooded, elm, ash, and Silver Maple may dominate the canopy while the understory vegetation would be shade-tolerant and rather limited in variety. In openings and around old river channels (oxbows), Buttonbush frequently forms impenetrable thickets right out into shallow waters. If spring floodwaters stand for weeks, as they often do in such situations, wild irises, arrowheads, various sedges, and bur-marigolds (beggar-ticks) may occur in small numbers or large stands. In better drained, well-lighted spots, Cardinalflower, Great Blue Lobelia, Skunk-cabbage, and Arrowhead may predominate. Later in the season, various sunflowers may light up the clearings and Wild-cucumber clambers over shrubby growth and up into small trees. Southward on drier soils at the upland edge of floodplain or on the sandier, somewhat higher riverbank levee itself, Green Dragon and Recurved or Prairie Trillium may be found. Nodding Trillium may occur very locally northward. On occasion, the Large White Trillium also appears. Some southern species which, in the heart of their range, occur in many upland habitats occur in our region mostly on suitable large river floodplains, although their incidence is rare (Twinleaf, Snow Trillium).

In general, however, floodplain vegetation is relatively uniform and of a limited number of species. As the season progresses, vast colonies of Stinging Nettles, Giant Ragweed, and Poison Ivy develop. Because this habitat is frequently mosquito ridden, not many people explore it thoroughly. Yet treasures may be found there throughout the growing season.

Skunk-cabbage
Symplocarpus foetidus
Arum Family

As early as late February, the flowering spadix of this species with its hooded spathe pokes through the snow cover in swamps, melting back the surrounding snow as its internal temperature increases. The first spring wildflower to bloom, Skunk-cabbage has contractile roots that are sensitive to temperature. On warm days, the roots take on water and expand, lifting the flower higher into the air. Conversely, on cold nights, the roots contract, pulling the flower lower into the warmer muck and thus reducing extensive frost damage. After flowering, large rhubarb-like, apple green leaves appear and remain throughout the growing season.

The skunk-like odor of the plant implied by its common name comes from crushed leaf and stem juices. The somewhat different odor of the flowers – more like putrid garbage than skunk – attracts carrion-loving insects and flies that emerge from hibernation in early spring. Following the odor to its source, they unintentionally pollinate the flowers. Also attractive to these insects is the maroon-mottled spathe.

Skunk-cabbage is found throughout the western Great Lakes region in black, mucky, springy soils although it is locally absent to the north. Like other members of the Jack-in-the-pulpit Family, its cells contain oxalic acid crystals. Humans biting into a plant will experience a stinging and burning sensation, although bears eat the plants and are reputed to have diminished local populations doing so.

fwc

Prairie Trillium; Toadshade
Trillium recurvatum
Lily Family

Prairie Trillium is a sessile trillium meaning its flowers sit directly on the leaves. Maroon or occasionally yellow, its 3 petals are clustered and upright atop the blotched or spotted leaves, and the sepals recurve downward against the stem. Unlike those of any other sessile trilliums in our area, the leaves of Prairie Trillium attach to the plant with petioles. Overall the plants appear tall and stiff and tend to form rather large colonies.

Found only in the southern and western portions of our region and rare here, Prairie Trillium is far more common southwest of the Great Lakes area. It prefers rich, calcareous, heavy soils, growing mainly on floodplain river banks, in low floodplain woods, or on lime rock hillsides.

Golden Ragwort

Senecio aureus
Aster or Daisy Family

From riches to rags, Golden Rag-wort matures from brilliant yellow flowers in April and May to white, fluffy fruits in June. This relative of the goldenrod produces clusters of small blossoms on stems 2 feet or more tall at a time when few other yellow composite flowers are in bloom. The plant typically forms colonies by underground runnners, and its non-flowering rhizomes produce glossy basal leaves.

A highly variable species, Golden Ragwort grows primarily in the spring-fed soil of damp, cool woods; on low grounds by rivers; and along calcareous, rocky shorelines. It ranges from Florida to Arkansas north to the Susquehanna River, Maryland, Kentucky, and Missouri.

Canada Anemone

Anemone canadensis
Buttercup Family

Canada Anemone is one of the showiest of our native anemones, both for its relatively large flowers and its tendency to form large showy colonies. Reaching heights up to 18 inches, the plants have lobed or cut leaves. Quarter-sized white blossoms appear in late May and early June on 12- to 20-inch stalks, the white parts being sepals rather than petals.

Ranging across Canada from Quebec to British Columbia south to New Jersey, Ohio, Missouri, and Kansas, Canada Anemone prefers sunny locations in wet meadows, on streambanks, and in roadside ditches. It may also be found along rocky lakeshores.

Green Dragon: Dragon-root
Arisaema dracontium
Arum Family

A member of the Jack-in-the-pulpit Family, Green Dragon is unique for its long, protruding, tongue-like spadix and its 5-parted rather than 3-parted leaves. Its spathe is entirely green, small, and closely wrapped around the flower axis that, pointed and tongue-like, extends well beyond the flowers. A late bloomer among native "Jacks," it typically flowers in June. Clusters of bright red berries follow the flowers, remaining on the plant until frost.

Green Dragon produces many offset plants from its stocky rhizome. Clumps of several large flowering stems surrounded by many small offset plants are common in heavy, low, alluvial soils. Of widespread local occurrence in the southern portion of our region, it is seldom seen, perhaps because its common associates are Poison Ivy, Stinging Nettle, and later in the season, Giant Ragweed. Further south, it is found from Florida across to Texas although it is increasingly uncommon throughout its range as a result of habitat loss.

Ground-cherry
Physalis longifolia
Nightshade Family

Grow near the ground its fruit does, but a "cherry" it is not. In fact, some members of this family are extremely poisonous if ingested. Certain Ground-cherries, however, are reportedly edible and are, in fact, appearing in produce sections of some supermarkets.

The nodding yellow and maroon flowers of this species with their united petals feature greatly inflated sepals that collectively resemble a small balloon enclosing a small, tomato-like yellow fruit. Flowering from June to August, this member of the family is not so conspicuous as the related cultivated Japanese Lantern. It ranges from Wyoming to Arizona and New Mexico east in bottomlands and may be found in or near cultivated fields.

Fringed Loosestrife
Lysimachia ciliata
Primrose Family

Fringed Loosestrife grows to 18 inches tall with an erect simple or branched stem. Its leaves are ovate or lanceolate and attach to the stem with fringed leaf stalks. Blooming from June to August, the slightly drooping, bright yellow flowers are star-like with 5 petals.

Preferring light shade, Fringed Loosestrife forms colonies in the borders of woodlands along floodplains, in low ground thickets, and in rich woods from Quebec to British Columbia and throughout most of the United States.

fwc

Swamp Rose
Rosa palustris
Rose Family

Clumps of upright, woody stems 3 to 5 feet tall with abundant, thin, sharp prickles on the stem characterize this plant, one predecessor of garden rose cultivars. Growing in areas often with shallow standing water (*palustris* means "of the swamps"), Swamp Rose produces one heavy flush of blooms per year in early summer. The usually rich pink blossoms have 5 crinkled pet- als and a sweet "rosey" fragrance. Red berry-like fruits (called hips) follow the blooms and often persist frozen and blackened throughout the winter.

Found in swamps, along shores of ponds and lakes, in damp thickets, and in bog borders, Swamp Rose ranges from Florida and Arkansas north to Minnesota and Quebec.

Michigan Lily; Turk's-cap Lily
Lilium michiganense
Lily Family

One of only two native lilies in the western Great Lakes region, Michigan Lily can attain heights over 6 feet. Its showy orange-red flowers bloom between late June and mid-July with 1 to 15 flowers on a single plant.

In addition to their brilliant color, the flowers are distinguishable by maroon spotting on the petals and extremely recurved sepals and petals. Stamens and pistils protrude forward from the sepals and petals allowing the flowers to be pollinated effectively by Swallowtail Butterflies.

Michigan Lily will grow both in sunny and shady locations on floodplains and streambanks, but it flowers more heavily and produces larger plants in full sun. Its range extends from Ontario and Manitoba south through Michigan to Tennessee and Kentucky.

Common Dodder
Cuscuta gronovii
Dodder Family

Common Dodder is a parasite on other plants. Notable for its lack of green color, Common Dodder begins life as a seed on the ground that germinates in the typical way. Once it achieves sufficient growth to reach a nearby plant however, it attaches to that plant by entwining around it and forming small projections that penetrate to the host's food tubes. When connection to the host is sufficient, the ground connection withers leaving a plant with masses of fleshy, almost fungus-like, orange-yellow stems. In mid- to late summer, small, white, star-like flowers develop along the stem.

Several of our dodder species are rare and endangered and a few can cause serious problems for other plants. This essentially harmless species grows on low ground near rivers and streams from Quebec to Manitoba south to Florida, Texas, and New Mexico.

Spotted Touch-me-not
Impatiens capensis
Touch-me-not Family

Thick, succulent, almost translucent fleshy stems expanded at the leaf joints are characteristic of this species. Plants 1 to 3 feet tall bear gently scallop-toothed leaves and, in late summer, delicate, trumpet-shaped flowers suspended by thread-like pedicels. A favorite of hummingbirds, the 2-lipped flowers with united petals are yellow with red spots and a curved spur at the back. The ripened pod-like fruits break apart explosively when touched – ultimately even without touching – thereby propelling seeds several feet. Ants and mice often bury numerous seeds resulting in distinctive germinating clumps the following spring.

Tolerating sunlight or shade, Spotted Touch-me-not is found in quite wet conditions, particularly in spring. It occurs in spongy ditches, meadows, forests, and hillside seeps across the north and southwest to Texas. Its stem juice is said to dry up Poison Ivy blisters.

Small Purple Fringed-orchid
Platanthera psycodes
Orchid Family

Small Purple Fringed-orchid occurs throughout the Great Lakes region where it can be locally rare or frequent in a given area. Somewhat fleshy-leaved plants 1 to 3 feet tall grow in a wide variety of habitats: in sunny wet meadows; along ditch banks and low lakeshores; and in elm-ash floodplain swamps, tag-alder thickets, and damp soil along trout streams. Northward, however, it occurs primarily in wet sunny meadows and on streambanks.

Depending on latitude and habitat, Small Purple Fringed-orchid will bloom at various times between June and August. Its flowering spikes can be densely packed and cylindrical with 30 to 70 flowers or loosely packed and lax with 8 to 25 blossoms. The two petals of each flower appear to be slightly chewed on the edges and project forward. Only the lip margins are shallowly cut or "fringed." Usually rose-purple in color, this native orchid occasionally occurs in pale lavender or pure white forms. In whatever color, they possess a delicately sweet fragrance.

This orchid species ranges from Newfoundland and Nova Scotia across to Quebec south through New York, New Jersey, Pennsylvania, and Virginia. Found also in the mountains of North Carolina and Georgia, it reaches as far west as Minnesota and Iowa in the Great Lakes region.

Wood Nettle
Laportea canadensis
Nettle Family

Although for different reasons, Wood Nettle, like *Impatiens capensis*, could also bear the common name Touch-me-not as one brush against its leaves will attest. Tiny hollow hairs on the leaves inject a substance into the skin that causes a painful stinging sensation that lasts several minutes.

Wood Nettle typically occurs in clusters of 5 to 8 stems. Up to 3 feet tall, the plants feature pale green leaves resembling those of the unrelated elm. Found from Quebec to Manitoba south to Florida and Oklahoma, this species tends to occur in densely shaded floodplain forest, especially around ponds or pools of standing water.

Groundnut; Wild-bean
Apios americana
Pea Family

Groundnut is a misnomer. Unlike its peanut cousin which matures its edible seeds (or "nuts") underground, the edible parts of this plant are the tuberous enlargements of its underground stems. For this reason, it is also commonly called Potato-bean. It was an important food of Native Americans.

A rapidly spreading, twining vine, Groundnut grows in wet, mucky soil in sun or shade, often overrunning and smothering neighboring vegetation. From July through September, it produces densely packed spikes of fleshy, hard-textured, dark brownish-rose flowers. Resembling sweet-pea blossoms in shape, they emit a scent of violet. Its area of distribution includes New Brunswick to Minnesota and Colorado south to Nova Scotia, New England, Long Island, Florida, Louisiana, and Texas.

Cardinal-flower; Red Lobelia
Lobelia cardinalis
Bellflower Family

One of the most aptly named wild-flowers, Cardinal-flower lives up to its common designation in July and August with dense spikes of vivid red blossoms. Each flower on the 16- to 30-inch spike is tubular and split at the top, the resulting 2 segments folded into lips. The upper lip is divided into 2 lobes spread almost like wings, and the lower lip has 3 lobes. Protruding between the lips is a reddish tube formed by the anther filaments, and extending through the center of that tube and beyond is a whitish or yellowish hook-like stigma.

Cardinal-flower is pollinated primarily by hummingbirds although bees also sometimes visit. As a hummingbird probes the nectar opening between the lips, the anthers shoot pollen out onto its beak, frequently leaving excess grains on the petals as well. As the flowers fade, a new rosette of flattened leaves forms at the base of the plant to persist throughout the winter. It will produce the next season's flowering stalk.

Although perennial, Cardinal-flower requires open, raw soil and freedom from competitive vegetation. New colonies frequently occur in recently cleared, sandy wet ditches only to disappear in a year or two as other vegetation invades. Found from Florida and Texas north to Michigan, Minnesota, and Quebec, it is very local in the upper part of our region and very widespread elsewhere in roadside ditches and other low, damp areas.

Great Blue Lobelia
Lobelia siphilitica
Bellflower Family

Like the related Cardinal-flower, Great Blue Lobelia may be found in waste places where the water table is high. However, it seems to have a wider tolerance of growing conditions than Cardinal-flower since it is more commonly found.

The flower structure of Great Blue Lobelia is very similar to that of Cardinal-flower, but the 3-foot plants are stockier and the flower spikes denser with their violet-blue, sky-blue, or white flowers from August to October. Generally pollinated by bees, it grows in swamps, meadows, and low rich woods and along streams and shores from the western edges of the Northeast to Minnesota and South Dakota south to eastern Virginia, the upland of North Carolina and Alabama, Mississippi, Missouri, and eastern Kansas.

87

Joe-pye-weed
Eupatorium maculatum
Aster or Daisy Family

Stems distinctly spotted with red-purple or purple throughout are characteristic of this tall, erect perennial of northern wet meadows and swampy roadsides and shorelines. Ovate, irregularly serrated leaves in whorls of 3, 4, and 5 occur at each node. Late summer brings flat-topped heads of pale pink to red-purple flowers with 9 to 22 florets per head. These flowering clusters are a real favorite of large butterflies.

Locally very abundant in the Great Lakes region, Joe-pye-weed ranges from Newfoundland to British Columbia south to New England, Pennsylvania, the mountains of North Carolina, Michigan, and northern Indiana into Iowa.

Boneset
Eupatorium perfoliatum
Aster or Daisy Family

Boneset is a relative of Joe-pye-weed and commonly grows with it in wet fields, swales, marshes, fens, and low clearings and on open riverbanks. A more delicate plant than its cousin, Boneset features a somewhat hairy stem and flat-topped heads of white to gray-white flowers from mid-July to September. Its unique leaf structure includes opposite leaves joined by their bases and encircling the stem as if the stem were inserted through the middle of a single leaf.

The common name of this plant likely refers back to the Doctrine of Signatures and the belief that the plant possessed properties beneficial in curing broken bones. It ranges from Quebec to Manitoba south to Florida, Louisiana, and Texas.

Turtlehead
Chelone glabra
Snapdragon Family

Related to snapdragons, Turtlehead is so named because its flower resembles the head of a turtle. Tubular in shape, the flowers have united petals and 2 small lips with a slightly open mouth, the lower lip featuring a white to pale yellow beard inside. Flower color is typically creamy white, rarely pinkish to greenish yellow. Ranked somewhat one above the other on a dense spike, the flowers open only a few buds at a time as early as late July and as late as October. Leaves are slightly toothed and opposite on the stem.

Turtlehead grows on low grounds and stream margins and in wet thickets. It occurs from Newfoundland, Ontario, and Minnesota south to Georgia, Alabama, and Missouri and is of infrequent occurrence in our region.

Virgin's Bower; Woodbine
Clematis virginiana
Buttercup Family

Virgin's Bower is the area's most common fall-blooming, white-flowered vine. With somewhat lobed, simple, 3-foliate leaves having few teeth, it attaches to other plants by bending or clasping of leaf stalks and can be seen clambering over nearby shrubs and thickets. In August and September, panicles of numerous creamy white flowers give the plants a frothy appearance. Single-sexed (dioecious), the mildly fragrant female flowers are followed by curly, woolly heads of tailed seeds that persist long into winter.

A plant of low ground, swampy woods, and streambanks, Virgin's Bower ranges from Quebec to Manitoba south to Georgia, Mississippi, Louisiana, and Kansas.

89

Wild-cucumber; Balsam-apple
Echinocystis lobata
Gourd Family

An annual vine with dark green, sharply 5-lobed leaves, Wild-cucumber is often seen along fences or climbing over other vegetation. As it climbs, it holds on by way of 3-forked, coiled tendrils – modified leaves or stems that aid grasping. In August and September in our region, separate erect clusters of male and female flowers appear on the vines. Flowers of both sexes are greenish white in color, the male flowers forming large, showy, erect clusters while the inconspicuous female flowers occur in small clusters or singly.

The fruits of Wild-cucumber are conspicuous and last well into winter. An ovoid dry capsule 2 to 3 inches long and 1 to 1½ inches in diameter, the fruit is very prickly. Openings in the ends of the capsules allow the discharge of large, flat seeds that produce the next year's crop of plants.

Wild-cucumber grows primarily in rich soil along streams and occasionally in ditches. Its range extends from New Brunswick to Saskatchewan south to Texas and Florida.

90

fwc

Michigan Holly;Winterberry
Ilex verticillata
Holly Family

Michigan Holly flowers in early summer, but we include it late because its fruits are far more conspicuous and easily recognized than its inconspicuous flowers.

A deciduous shrub of variable size, Michigan Holly grows mostly in acid swamps, often in standing water; on low ground and streambanks; and in bog borders. Its dark green leaves are simple, mostly alternate, lanceolate, and fine-toothed. Dull above, they have conspicuous recessed veins. The flowers are tiny and green to white in color. Occurring on short stalks and in clusters, they have 5- to 8-parted pet-

als. Separate sexes occur on separate plants, so both male and female plants must be nearby to cross-pollinate and produce fruits.

The brilliant red fruits of Michigan Holly appear before the leaves fall and may persist well into winter if not eaten by birds. These fleshy fruits with several hard seeds can be extremely showy in good years.

Michigan Holly is found from Newfoundland to Minnesota south to Georgia, Tennessee, and Illinois and is protected against commercial cutting in Michigan.

Northern Coniferous Forest

The northern coniferous or boreal forest is a climax-like formation that occurs in the northernmost portions of the Great Lakes region. Influenced by the cooling effects of the lakes, our latitude, and the short growing season, this plant formation is cooler and wetter than the deciduous forest or Beech-Sugar Maple forest to its south. Much of the soil on which it occurs is sandy or derived from sandstones or granites. Such soils, characteristically acidic, are further acidified by the decomposing needles and litter of the dominant conifers. Because most conifers are evergreen, the cooling effect of the climate is enhanced by the heavy shade. In these cool conditions, decay of needles and leaves is retarded and deep layers of moisture-retaining, acid humus accumulate. In some areas, pine needle litter and accumulated humus virtually smother most herbaceous growth.

As with other formations, as one moves northward, the change is somewhat gradual from deciduous to northern coniferous woodland. At first, there is an increase in hemlock in ravines and on northern slopes. Gradually, White Cedar (*Thuja occidentalis*), Balsam Fir (*Abies balsamea*), and White Spruce (*Picea glauca*) appear on northern slopes or in moisture-cooled swampland borders. Farther north, near Lake Superior and in northern Ontario, pioneer forests of aspen, birch, Red Maple, and scattered oaks develop an understory of Balsam Fir. Gradually the firs overtop and supplant the deciduous species. However, in northern Michigan and Wisconsin, fully developed northern coniferous forest occurs only along the Lake Superior shores, on headlands and offshore islands, in bits and pieces in cold or unusually shaded pockets, or in the understory of northern treed fens where the shade of White Cedar, Balsam Fir, and spruces dominates. Only on the Canadian shore of Lake Superior and northward, on Isle Royale, or in extreme northern Minnesota does the true northern coniferous forest develop fully within our region.

fwc

In the cool shade of the conifers on the deep acidic humus, the number of herbaceous plant species may be limited. What the area may lack in species variety may be countered in numbers however. A ground cover of Bunchberry or Twinflower may extend over acres or even many square miles. Canada Mayflower forms large patches in the damp humus. Goldthread, Star-flower, and Pink Lady's-slippers abound. Local colonies of various rattlesnake plantains, Bluebead-lily, and Fringed Polygala dot the landscape. North of our region or extremely locally in bog borders or on headlands, Upland Cranberry or Lingonberry may predominate. Numerous small, often green-flowered orchids appear – rein-orchids (*Platantheras*), coral-roots (*Corallorhizas*), and twayblades (*Listeras*).

As in all regions, not only are there species unique to the northern coniferous forest, but even the dominant species in the bogs or other wetlands of the region may differ, or the proportion of one species to another may differ from that of bogs farther south. Species of this forest, demanding cool soils but indifferent to moisture, may occupy shaded cold bogs far south of this forest. Thus one may find Bluebead-lily or Bunchberry in a heavily shaded bog forest in southern Michigan or northern Indiana, surviving as relicts in the cool soils in regions where they could not survive on the uplands they dominate farther north.

Most wildflowers of the northern coniferous forest have vast ranges. Many occur across the entire North American continent, some across Europe and Asia as well. Some grow throughout the eastern portion of the northern coniferous forest from Manitoba to Newfoundland. A few may occur only in very limited areas, but these are exceptions.

Calypso; Fairy Slipper
Calypso bulbosa
Orchid Family

Very rare and local in our region, Calypso occasionally ventures out of swamps (see also under Great Lakes Shorelines and Dunes) to cool upland positions and deeply shaded moist depressions in northern coniferous forests. Further north it becomes more tolerant of drier locations and more widespread.

Aptly named for the islandic goddess in *The Odyssey* whose beauty made men forget home and family, this tiny, delicate orchid typically occurs in colonies of a few individual plants. Although potentially long-lived, its habit of growing in short-lived or fragile substrates – such as moss beds and decaying logs – often dooms it to early death sometimes hastened by careless hikers, offroad vehicles, lumbering, and effects of other human activity.

Twinflower
Linnaea borealis
Honeysuckle Family

The flowers of this trailing vine were the favorite of famed Swedish botanist Carl Linnaeus for whom it is named. Flat with somewhat hairy opposite-paired leaves, Twinflower creeps over the ground, covering extensive areas in cool, northern woodlands. United twin flowers, pale to deep pink, dangle from threadlike, 5-inch branched stems in June and July. The delicately fragrant blossoms feature united petals with pointed tips, the petals forming a tube filled inside with pink hairs.

Found throughout the world in the far north, Twinflower is locally abundant on drier hummocks of cedar swamps and northern coniferous forest of the northern Great Lakes region. It also occurs farther south locally on mountains and in cool bogs.

Naked Miterwort
Mitella nuda
Saxifrage Family

A denizen of cool depressions in coniferous woods or cool swamps, this tiny plant is small enough to be lost under the leaves of Bluebead-lily. Up to 5 inches tall, Naked Miterwort plants have only basal leaves, the latter distinguishable by their erect hairs. Greenish-yellow to bronze flowers occur loosely scattered along leafless flower stalks – hence the common name of the species. Blooming from May to June, the tiny flowers feature featherlike petals that give the blossoms a snowflake appearance.

Naked Miterwort ranges from the Canadian Northwest to Newfoundland south to Pennsylvania, Ohio, and Minnesota.

97

Canada Mayflower
Maianthemum canadense
Lily Family

A colony of heart-shaped leaves from creeping underground stems makes Canada Mayflower conspicuous on the spring floor of moist woodland habitats. The main stems of flowering plants bear 2 or 3 leaves, those of non-blooming plants only 1 large leaf. Small cylindrical spikes of 15 to 30 tiny, fragrant white flowers shaped like miniature lilies appear above the leaves in May and June. A unique feature of this plant is the occurrence of flower parts in multiples of 2 rather than 3 as is typical of most Lily Family members. The flowers are followed in fall by berries that are first green, then mottled pink, and finally a brilliant red above the withering leaves. Like many fruits of the Lily Family, the berries may be poisonous.

Canada Mayflower grows in dense colonies that often do not persist long in a given spot. Found across the continent, it prefers acid soils.

98

Bluebead-lily; Lemon-lily; Clintonia
Clintonia borealis
Lily Family

Bluebead-lily is one of a limited number of *Clintonia* species found in North America. Spread by underground runners (stolons), it forms large colonies of plants in the cool, shady, humus-rich soils to which it is confined. Blooming plants feature 3 distinctive, large, fleshy leaves. Often mistaken for those of native orchids, the leaves differ from our orchids in possessing tiny silken hairs along their edges. From May to August, 3 to 5 lemon-yellow flowers top each 14-inch stem. Late in the growing season, this beauty produces large, shiny, dark blue-violet berries that are non-edible for humans.

In our region, Bluebead-lily occurs in coniferous forests to the north and in the cool drier edges of bogs to the south. It is especially abundant in the Lake Superior district on wet or dry soils.

Star-flower
Trientalis borealis
Primrose Family

A relative of the primrose, Star-flower spreads by underground runners to form plants with a single whorl of 5 to 7 pointed leaves. Between May and July, delicate, elongated flower stalks grow from the whorl of leaves, each producing 1 to 3 erect white flowers with 5 to 7 pointed petals united at their base. The flat, star-like corolla falls intact to the ground after pollination.

Star-flower is widely distributed from Labrador to Saskatchewan south to Newfoundland, Nova Scotia, New England, Virginia, W. Virginia, Ohio, Illinois, and Minnesota. Local but not rare in the Great Lakes region, it can be found in cool woods almost anywhere in the north and in the drier edges of bogs southward.

jrw

Painted Trillium
Trillium undulatum
Lily Family

Painted Trillium reaches its westward extension in southwestern Ontario and extreme eastern Michigan. Its strongly petioled leaves feature a distinctive pointed tip and less prominent veins than those in other trilliums of our region. At flowering the green color of the leaves displays a bronzy undertone.

The last of the trilliums to bloom in a given area, Painted Trillium emerges from the ground to a height of a few inches with a small open flower. Continuing to expand rapidly for a couple of days, it may become as tall as 15 inches with a blossom 3 inches across if not pollinated. Petals of pollinated flowers quickly wither and fall.

Thin-textured with wavy margins, each white petal features a red marking in the shape of a "V" and red veins near its base. In mid-summer, erect, somewhat cylindrical scarlet berries follow the flowers.

Painted Trillium is a plant of intensely acid, cool soils rich in humus. Rare within its limited range in the Great Lakes region, it will be found in coniferous woods; in cool, moist White Pine/Red Maple woods; and occasionally in bog margins in the north. It is more common in the high mountains of the southern Appalachians. Extremely difficult to move or cultivate, it should be enjoyed only in the wild.

Striped Coral-root
Corallorhiza striata
Orchid Family

Spotted Coral-root
Corallorhiza maculata
Orchid Family

Coral-roots derive their common name from their clusters of fleshy underground stems resembling coral. The name is somewhat misleading though as they lack roots. Devoid of chlorophyll, both species have leaves reduced to scales. Long thought to feed on decayed matter, coral-roots are now known to be indirect parasites that attach to their host by a slave fungus.

Striped Coral-root is the showiest of all coral-roots and the first to bloom of the two here discussed. Found singly or in clusters, it grows from 6 inches to 2 feet tall. Its red to pink flowering stem is surrounded by a yellow-pink basal sheath and is leafless. It produces a dense spike of maroon-striped pink blossoms in May and June. Pendant and boat-shaped, the lip of this orchid appears ruby red in sunlight. After maturation and pollination, individual flowers begin to droop, resulting in fruits that hang downward toward the ground.

Two forms of Spotted Coral-root grow in our region, both producing one to many slender, brownish or reddish leafless stalks 10 to 18 inches tall. Primarily of western distribution, the one shown here has established itself mostly in northern coniferous forests and dry Alder-Balsam Fir woods near the upper Great Lakes shores and ocasionally in cold, inland cedar fens. It is the earlier blooming of the two forms in a given region, usually flowering in June to early July. With a greater tendency to clump, this early form also produces a denser head of more flowers, each similar to a tropical orchid bloom in miniature. Its white, purple-spotted lip bears a smaller lobe on each side and is flared into a widened wavy top. Sepals and petals form a palm-like overhang to the lip.

Thimbleberry
Rubus parviflorus
Rose Family

The species name *parviflorus* is a misnomer for this plant. *Parva* means small, but this species produces the largest flowers of our native raspberries. Occurring in clusters, the 5-petaled white flowers open 1 or 2 at a time from globular, hairy buds in June and July. Although this species is native to cold climates, its flower buds are sensitive to low temperatures and therefore need the insulation of heavy snows in order to bloom.

Ripe Thimbleberries are rich carmine red in color. The thimble-shaped fruit actually consists of many 1-seeded fruits grouped together. Because the tissue below the berry remains on the plant, the berry is hollow whereas in blackberries that tissue comes off with the fruits and the berries are therefore solid. Thimbleberries are widely used for jellies and tarts despite their being seedy and not particularly juicy or sweet.

A weakly woody, thornless shrub with large maple-like leaves, Thimbleberry spreads by root runners into large colonies in cool soils, forming thickets on the woodland floor. Found from the Bruce Peninsula in Ontario to Minnesota in the upper Great Lakes, it is primarily of western distribution where it ranges from Mexico to Alaska and Alberta.

fwc

jrw

103

Bunchberry; Canada Dogwood
Cornus canadensis
Dogwood Family

Bunchberry is one of the most frequently encountered ground covers of the northern coniferous forest across the continent. Although individuals may attain heights of 10 inches or so, the average for this floppy-stemmed perennial is perhaps half that. At the tops of the stems, 2 to 3 pairs of leaves grow at 90 degrees from each other so closely together that they give the false impression of being whorled. Like the leaves of all members of its genus, those of Bunchberry display deeply engraved veins on their upper surfaces. An additional 1 to 2 pairs of small leaves may be found farther down the stem.

Produced from May through July, the flowers of this species consist of 2 pairs of white false petals (modified leaves) surrounding a cluster of small green flowers bearing minute true petals. Beginning in July and lasting into October, the spherical clusters of fleshy red fruits ripen. Equally as showy as the white floral bracts, they present a striking contrast against the summer green and often mahogany fall color of the leaves.

Bunchberry ranges widely across Canada and the northern and eastern United States.

104

Green Pyrola; Green Shinleaf
Pyrola chlorantha
Shinleaf or Wintergreen Family

Pink Pyrola; Pink Shinleaf
Pyrola asarifolia
Shinleaf or Wintergreen Family

Characteristic of cool, northern coniferous woods, pyrolas thrive in dark, mossy habitats scattered with pine needles where little else grows. Although some western species of this family produce leafless flowering plants lacking chlorophyll, ours usually display leaves and are green. More or less circular in shape, the glossy, evergreen leaves occur in basal rosettes produced from creeping underground stems. Five-petaled flowers are borne above the leaves on a scaly scape that arises from the rosette, each blossom attached by an individual stalk to the scape, much like the flowers of Lily-of-the-valley.

The leaves of Green Pyrola are rather small and leathery, forming a compact rosette. Its 5- to 10-inch scapes produce 2 to 13 yellow-green flowers that open to a bell shape. It grows in drier bog edges as well as coniferous woods from Labrador to Alaska south to Massachusetts, Wisconsin, and Arizona, flowering typically in June and July.

Pink Pyrola features larger leaves that aren't as leathery. Its longer leaf stalks give the rosette a rangier appearance compared to Green Pyrola. With 1 to 3 almost translucent bracts along its length, the scape reaches heights of 6 to 15 inches and bears 4 to 22 blossoms, also bell-shaped, in crimson to pale pink. Found across Canada south into New England, New York, Indiana, and Wisconsin and as far south as New Mexico in the Rocky Mountains, Pink Pyrola prefers moist calcareous soils and flowers in July and August.

105

One-flowered Shinleaf
Moneses uniflora
Shinleaf or Wintergreen Family

The complex flowers of this circumboreal species feature a distinctive structure. Green-white to white petals surround a large apple green ovary with a thickened, enlarged stigma and the tips of the anthers diverging like horns from the blossom. Hanging flowers occur from June to August on a scape 2 to 5 inches tall emerging from a rosette of crinkly, dark green leaves widely spaced at ground level. Seed capsules are upright.

One-flowered Shinleaf occupies forest niches where other green plants don't grow – in deep shade, moss, and sometimes pine litter. Absent in the south of our region, it is found in central districts almost exclusively in bogs because it requires cool soil. Northward it also grows on cold lakeshores and in dry coniferous forests.

Pipsissewa; Prince's-pine
Chimaphila umbellata
Shinleaf or Wintergreen Family

This low evergreen perennial reproduces vegetatively by means of underground stems, each "plant" thus being an aerial shoot up to 10 inches tall. Green and glossy on their upper surfaces, the leaves of Pipsissewa are wedge-shaped and toothed, occurring in whorls or scattered on the stem. Pink and white flowers appear in July and August displaying a large green ovary with a depression containing the sunken stigma. Usually hanging, the blossoms occur in an umbel resembling those of the shinleafs. The fruits are upright.

Once used for Christmas greens, Pipsissewa is now protected in some states, but a greater threat to its survival is loss of habitat. The several varieties of this plant range across the continent in cold, northern coniferous forests. A spotted-leaved southern species, *C. maculata*, has been reported more frequently in our region of late.

Pine-drops
Pterospora andromedea
Indian-pipe Family

Pine-drops is memorable for its height – more than 2 feet; its stout, wand-like stem with many scale-like leaves; and its red-purple-brown color. Hairy in appearance, clammy to the touch, and lacking chlorophyll, it is parasitic on the roots of nearby trees. From June to August, the stems produce fleshy white to reddish flask-shaped blossoms that droop in a many-flowered raceme. Old seed-bearing stems of this species may persist for several years.

Pine-drops prefers dry, basic soils of pine forests and ranges across Canada south to Vermont, New York, Michigan, Wisconsin, and through the Rocky Mountains to Mexico. It is quite rare in our region.

Creeping Rattlesnake Plantain
Goodyera repens
Orchid Family

The smallest of the rattlesnake plantains and the only one found around the world in the northern hemisphere, this species forms small colonies in the deep shade of coniferous woods and bogs, its branching stems arising at the surface of moss carpets. The evergreen leaves of the North American variety (var. *repens*) are marked with silver-green veins that give it a snake-like appearance. Flower scapes up to 10 inches tall bear 10 to 20 blossoms in late July and August. Crystalline white and pubescent, the flowers all face only one direction. Each flower's lowermost petal, the lip, is pouched at the base, boat-shaped, and pointed at the tip.

Creeping Rattlesnake Plaintain grows most abundantly in the Lake Superior region. Its range extends as far south as the high mountains of the Carolinas in the east and New Mexico in the west.

107

Ponds and Marshes

fwc

fwc

Ponds can refer to rather small, shallow bodies of water or, as in New England, to most inland lakes, even those of considerable acreage and depth. Herein we refer to ponds as bodies of water usually of less than several acres, only a few feet deep, and often with levels fluctuating considerably as a result of changes in season and rainfall amounts. Pond margins are usually free of significant wave action and hence quite still-watered. There are a few, but not many, aquatic plants found exclusively around pond margins in our area. Most pond-border plants here are found also in various other wetlands – marshes, swamps, streambanks, and shallows.

Marshes are variously defined by different authors. One definition of a marsh is "a wet area with slow but definite drainage, usually with standing water and cat-tail or rush-like emergent vegetation dominating and with few or no trees." Marshes can exist as a single environmental feature, or marsh vegetation can develop around a large shallow pond. Vegetation can range from plants demanding the quiet water of the pond to others adapted to the slow marsh drainage and further to those requiring the more rapidly moving stream current. In the region of this book, large marshes formerly occurred on the lake plain margins of Lakes Erie and Huron, especially Saginaw Bay, and locally on southern Lake Michigan.

Marsh waters, by definition, slowly drain, so some decaying plant matter is constantly removed from the marsh. Because moving water usually contains some oxygen, partial decay of dead plant matter occurs, leaving only small amounts of plant matter to accumulate and form peat. Marshes therefore usually have a mucky, somewhat peaty floor mixed with flood deposits of min-

110

fwc

eral soil. Drained and plowed, such soils are considerably fertile. Much of our former lake plain marsh is today diked and farmed. One estimate suggests that over 90 percent of such land is now under cultivation.

Bits and pieces of true marshland still occur along the Great Lakes, and small riverbank and other inland marshlands still exist. In places, seepage fens grade on their downhill side into pond border or inland marsh. Thus, as stated earlier, various plants listed here as marsh and pond margin plants may also be encountered in other wetland habitats.

Ponds and marshes, like all habitats, undergo natural successional development. However, the slow current in marsh waters in combination with flooding and fluctuations in Great Lakes and water table levels has the effect of slowing or even temporarily reversing the successional process. So natural marsh changes are somewhat cyclic – developing, being destroyed, and then redeveloping.

Some plants of these habitats show tissue adaptations to conduct air to their roots. Most utilize water movement to disperse seeds. Some have both floating, aquatic leaves and in drier situations, aerial leaves. Only a few have flowers that float on the water surface, while still fewer submerged, delicate water plants utilize the water surface and floating pollen as a means of pollination of their flowers. Many have showy insect-pollinated flowers.

Marsh-marigold; Cowslip
Caltha palustris
Buttercup Family

A long-lived perennial, Marsh-marigold is one of our region's largest members of the Buttercup Family and one of the earliest to bloom. Its lush, dark green, almost circular, cleft leaves form a striking background to the large, bright yellow blossoms. In April and May in our region, the 1- to 2-foot plants bear few to many flowers on stiffly branched stalks. Glistening yellow and petal-like, the sepals give the flowers their color and cup shape, for true petals do not occur in this plant.

Marsh-marigold grows generally in standing shallow water and springy seeps and on wet banks and hills. Found worldwide in the north, its North American range extends from Labrador to Alaska south to Newfoundland, South Carolina, Tennessee, Iowa, and Nebraska.

112

Yellow Water Crowfoot
Ranunculus flabellaris
Buttercup Family

Yellow Water Crowfoot is an amphibious plant capable of surviving and reproducing in aquatic sites, but it can also grow successfully on moist soils. The leaves of submerged plants are very delicate like those of aquarium plants. On land, the leaves are smaller and thicker. Typical buttercup flowers borne just above the water appear in May and June, sometimes in numbers large enough to give the appearance of a floating yellow carpet. Clusters of small, beaked, nutlet fruits follow.

This species occurs from Maine to British Columbia south to North Carolina, Louisiana, Kansas, and into the western mountains.

Yellow Flag
Iris pseudacorus
Iris Family

Our only yellow "wild" iris, Yellow Flag is a European garden escape now widely spread in the Great Lakes region and elsewhere. Its bright green, 3- to 4-foot leaves are spear-like with 2 ridges. Flower stalks can be 3 to 5 feet tall, bearing brilliant canary yellow blossoms from May to July.

Yellow Flag often grows in standing water that is sometimes fairly deep. It is most frequently seen in the shallow waters of larger rivers and along lakeshores including those of the Great Lakes. Moist prairies and meadows are less common habitats.

fwc

Wild Blue Flag; Wild Iris
Iris versicolor
Iris Family

Wild Blue Flag is one of two Great Lakes iris species that appear similar to each other, the second being *I. virginica* commonly known as Southern Blue Flag. As evidenced by the common name of the latter, Wild Blue Flag is the more northern species, occurring mostly in the northern half of our coverage area. Where the two grow together, they are distinguishable by several traits. Most notably, Wild Blue Flag flowers well above the foliage while the flowers of the southern species are at or below the foliage tips . In addition, the colors of the leaf bases and sepals differ. Our Blue Flag has purplish leaf bases and greenish-yellow sepal bases while the corresponding colors in Southern Blue Flag are brown or tan and bright yellow. Hybridization between the two can, however, create identification problems.

A plant of damp soil near ponds, along streambanks, and in marshes, bog borders, and northern fens, Wild Blue Flag occurs from Labrador to Manitoba south to West Virginia, northern Ohio, Michigan, Wisconsin, and Minnesota. It flowers from May to August in color forms from blue to white, and plants can vary from 2 to 4 feet in height depending on soil fertility and moisture.

White Water-lily
Nymphaea odorata
Water-lily Family

White Water-lily is the only native white-flowered water-lily south of the northern Lake Superior region. Its numerous petals and bright yellow stamens are distinctive, but the fragrance of the mature flowers distinguish it from all other similar species.

A plant of quiet waters, White Water-lily features large leaves arising from underwater horizontal stems. Purple to maroon on their undersides, the leaves typically float on top of the water. Flowering occurs from June to September but is heaviest at the first flush. In acid bog pools and other extreme growing conditions, the flowers may be dwarfed, but in rich, fertile water they can be 5 to 6 inches across.

Considered by some authorities to encompass two species in our region (*N. odorata* and *N. tuberosa*), White Water-lily grows throughout northeast North America south to the Gulf Coast.

Arrowhead; Duck-potato

Sagittaria latifolia
Water-plantain Family

Distinctive arrowhead-shaped leaves are the hallmark of this shallow water plant. Quite variable in size and shape on the same plant in different seasons, the leaves are usually broad though very narrow-leaved forms occur. The common name Duck-potato derives from the plant's fleshy underwater food storage structures, a favorite food of dabbling ducks.

Arrowhead blooms more or less all summer on stems 1 to 3 feet tall. The showy 3-petaled white flowers occur in whorls at intervals up the stem with the lower flowers predominantly female.

Found from New Brunswick to British Columbia south to South Carolina, Alabama, Louisiana, Oklahoma, and California, it grows in the shallow water of ponds, ditches, lakeshores, and streams.

Bur-reed

Sparganium eurycarpum
Bur-reed Family

The Bur-reed Family is an important food source for water fowl, and this species is probably our region's most common family member. Soft, ribbon-like leaves trail downstream from plants in deep moving water. In shallow water, it bears emergent leaves resembling those of the Iris Family. From spring to early summer, flowers ripen from bottom to top scattered along sparingly branched stems with long, leaf-like bracts. Large, round, and showy, 2 or 3 female flowers occur near each bract. Deriving their color from fleshy white stigmas, the female flowers ripen into firm round fruits, the stigmas persisting as dried spines and giving the plant the name Bur-reed. Short-lived staminate (male) flower heads occur further up the stem.

Bur-reed ranges from eastern Canada to Alaska and British Columbia south to Florida, Kansas, Colorado, Utah, and California.

Swamp Milkweed
Asclepias incarnata
Milkweed Family

Swamp Milkweed shares its distinctive flower structure with all other milkweeds. Occurring in umbrella-shaped umbels of several per stem, individual flowers display an outside ring (corona) of cup-shaped or hood-like structures surrounding the stamen tube, each with a small horned tooth. Below these structures are 5-parted petals usually reflexed downward and away from the corona. In this species, the rose pink to purple flowers bloom from June to August.

Our only milkweed that may grow in standing water, Swamp Milkweed occurs as solitary stems up to 4 feet tall or in clumps. Its narrow leaves are more willow-like than those of its relatives and contain little of the milky sap characteristic of the family. It typically grows at the edges of ponds and streams from Quebec to Wyoming south to Texas, Louisiana, Tennessee, and South Carolina. Off-white forms occur rarely.

Flowering-rush
Butomus umbellatus
Flowering-rush Family

Semi-aquatic to aquatic, tall, and reed-like, Flowering-rush is a dangerously aggressive Eurasian introduction that is spreading throughout the northeastern United States in shallow water. Between June and September, it produces flowering umbels with widely radiating pedicels, each bearing an individual flower with 3 relatively large deep pink petals. Although flowers are individually small (up to 1 inch across), collectively they can be quite showy. Leaves are narrow and triangular, and the underground tubers are a food source for wild game birds.

Found in muddy soils as well as shallow water, Flowering-rush is common in Lakes Erie and St. Clair and continues to spread northward and westward in our region.

118

Willow-weed; Nodding Smartweed
Polygonum lapathifolium
Smartweed Family

The two common names of this annual plant provide keys to its identifying characteristics. The leaves of the many-branched weed are somewhat erect and willow-like, their point of attachment to the stem being swollen like those of most members of the family. From late summer into fall, its white to pink flowers occur in limp, densely packed cylindrical spikes that arch or nod.

Reaching heights up to 6 feet, Willow-weed often forms large patches in swampy thickets, on damp shores and streambanks, and at pond margins from Newfoundland to British Columbia south to New Jersey, Pennsylvania, South Dakota, and California. Both native and introduced forms occur.

Water Smartweed
Polygonum amphibium
Smartweed Family

Both terrestrial and aquatic forms of this species occur in the Great Lakes region. The terrestrial form grows only in the southern portion while the aquatic form pictured is found throughout the region and is the only smartweed seen northward.

Water Smartweed's long, willow-like, floating leaves may be green to maroon-red. The plants themselves are smooth if in water but hairy out of water. Flower spikes are dense, tapered cylinders that sit erect just above the water from 1 to 4 inches.

Found throughout the world in the far north, Water Smartweed grows from Labrador to Alaska south to Ohio, Indiana, and Colorado and often occurs in such large colonies as to color the surface of a pond pink for an acre or more.

119

Flat-leaved Bladderwort
Utricularia intermedia
Bladderwort Family

A circumpolar species, Flat-leaved Bladderwort can grow in muddy sites as well as in water of varying depths. According to Voss' *Michigan Flora* (1997), it thrives and blooms best in shallow water.

The leaves of this carnivorous aquatic species are very thin, fan-shaped, and green with branches that bear large numbers of microscopic bladders about $1/32$ inch wide. The bladder-traps are bag-shaped vacuums with trigger mechanisms. When the triggers are touched by microscopic aquatic animals, the bladders rupture, sucking in the victim and surrounding material. Digestion of usuable organisms within this material provides nutrients for the plant. Dark colored bladders have already trapped, clear colored have not.

The flowers of Flat-leaved Bladderwort are bright yellow, and large numbers of blooming plants often render extensive portions of ponds that color between May and September. Somewhat snapdragon-like with two lips, the blossoms rise above the water on slender stalks. Unlike the humped lower lip of the related Common Bladderwort, the lower lip of this species is almost flat, and the flower bears a spur that bends under and presses against that lip.

Found primarily in alkaline waters of shallow pools, marshes, ponds, lakes, and fens, Flat-leaved Bladderwort extends from Greenland to Newfoundland and Alaska down to Long Island, Delaware, Ohio, Illinois, and California.

fwc

Pond-lily; Cow-lily; Spatterdock
Nuphar variegata
Water-lily Family

Sometimes referred to as Cow-lily, Pond-lily is a good example of several species that occur in our area. The plants arise from a massive system of roots often 5 inches or more in diameter. Waxy and oval, the leaves float or sit semi-erect just above the water on rather thick stalks. Underground stems are covered with leaf scars resembling pocks and filled with spongy tissue that conducts air.

Yellow, sometimes with a greenish base, Pond-lily flowers are cup-shaped with 5 or 6 sepals as opposed to the numerous, long, pointed petals of white water-lilies. Also rising above the water on stiff stalks, Pond-lily flowers appear throughout most of the summer. This species ranges from Labrador to Alaska south to Nebraska, South Dakota, Florida, and Texas.

fwc

Tufted Loosestrife
Lysimachia thyrsiflora
Primrose Family

Found especially in shallow waters of ponds and lakes, Tufted Loosestrife takes its species name *thyrsiflora* from the arrangement of its flowers – in a thyrse, i.e. clusters extending from a single main axis like grapes or lilacs. Yellow and somewhat fuzzy with dark dots, they occur in the axils of the leaves from May to July. The plants themselves are 2 to 3 feet tall with herbaceous stems and willow-like leaves. Arising from underground creeping stems, they can form colonies in marshy habitats from Quebec to Alaska south to West Virginia, Indiana, Missouri, and California.

False Loosestrife; Seedbox
Ludwigia alternifolia
Evening-primrose Family

A rare plant of wet, sandy regions, False Loosestrife grows 1 to 3 feet tall and features smooth, alternating, semi-aquatic leaves pointed at both ends. Flowers occur from June to August with 5 conspicuous yellow petals. The distinctive cubical seed capsules are rounded at the base and open by a terminal pore.

Found in swamps and frequently on disturbed wet sandy soils, False Loosestrife grows from Florida to Texas north to Massachusetts, New York, Michigan, and Kansas.

Purple Loosestrife
Lythrum salicaria
Loosestrife Family

An introduction from Europe, Purple Loosestrife has literally taken over shorelines of lakes, ponds, and streams throughout northeast Canada and the United States. One of our showiest summer flowers used as a garden perennial, it unfortunately is an aggressive colonizer that escapes into natural habitats where it rapidly becomes dominant, displacing many to all native species in the process. One effective remedy found thus far is to flood the affected area deeply for a period of time, a technique that also destroys all other native vegetation. Current hopes for eradication rest on an insect parasite recently introduced into the region. Despite its beauty and hardiness, this plant should not be purchased or planted in the garden. Minnesota, in fact, has outlawed its sale.

Purple Loosestrife typically grows in clumps of many erect stems up to 4½ to 5 feet tall. Plants are somewhat downy with lanceolate leaves that are heart-shaped at the base. Tall spikes bearing many 5-petaled magenta or pink flowers provide a striking display in late summer.

124

Rose Mallow; Swamp Mallow
Hibiscus moscheutos
Mallow Family

This shrubby-appearing relative of the hollyhock is actually a very large herb rather than a woody plant. From late July to September, Rose Mallow is readily identifiable by clusters of very large, usually pink, hollyhock-style flowers on bushy plants. Deep rose and cream colored forms, the latter with a red base, occur more rarely.

Reaching heights up to 6 feet, the plant is almost furry. Lower leaves have 3 lobes while upper leaves are unlobed, but both display a faint whitish velvety coating on the underside.

Rose Mallow is primarily a coastal plain plant of the eastern United States and southern Ontario, but it also is found in marshes of Lake Erie and southern Lake Michigan as well as adjacent inland areas. Within its limited range in our region, Rose Mallow is quite rare due to habitat disappearance although horticultural forms are readily available. In Michigan it is a plant of concern; in Ontario it is listed as vulnerable.

125

American Lotus
Nelumbo lutea
Water-lily Family

Our region's only apparently native lotus, American Lotus has become very rare and local in the Great Lakes area since the introduction of carp that eat the roots and seeds of the plants. Where it survives, large colonies form from branching runners underwater and in the mud below water. In the fall, the terminal bud and about 1 foot of the stem behind it form a brittle banana-like tuber that winters over. Both the tuber and seeds are reputed to be highly edible. In fact, some believe the plant may have been introduced to our area as a food plant by Native Americans.

American Lotus produces 2 types of leaves, the earlier ones floating with a leaf stalk attached in the center. In the latter half of the season just before the flowers bloom, the plant produces larger leaves up to umbrella-sized and standing up to 2 feet above water with centers depressed or cupped. Both leaf types lack the characteristic slit of water-lily leaves.

American Lotus bears flowers on separate stalks among and above the leaves from July to September. Pale yellow and up to a foot across, they have numerous concave petals. In their centers are numerous anthers plus a flat-toped receptacle containing separate ovaries in individual chambers. The ovaries eventually develop into nut-like seeds. The receptacle forms a dried pod that is frequently used in floral arrangements.

A plant of ponds and quiet streams, American Lotus ranges from Florida to Texas and north locally to southern New England, New York, southern Ontario, Minnesota, and Iowa.

fwc

Wild-rice
Zizania aquatica
Grass Family

This shallow water grass prefers slowly moving or non-stagnant water, usually under 2 feet deep, with a muddy or silty bottom. It does not compete with other plants and may occur as single plants or in large stands. An annual plant, it grows from seed to fruit and dies in a single season. While the individual flowers are not showy, the Wild-rice flower cluster is noteworthy. The female (pistillate) flowers are lowermost, the male flowers closely grouped above. The highly edible seeds comprise a major food of wildlife and originally of Native Americans. Today, wild rice cultivation is a considerable industry in Wisconsin and Minnesota.

Though Wild-rice is still widespread in our region, its habitat has suffered disturbance and destruction from "lakeshore improvement" projects.

Pickerel-weed
Pontederia cordata
Pickerel-weed Family

One of the showiest aquatic plants, Pickerel-weed inhabits ponds, lakeshore shallows, and marshes throughout our area, usually in waters less than 2 feet deep but occasionally deeper. Forming a clump of stems, each bearing a spear-shaped or somewhat elongated heart-shaped leaf rounded at the tip, the plant bears, above each leaf, a dense, spike-like inflorescence. Each day over a period of a week or two in mid- to late summer, a series of small, blue to lavendar-blue, two-lipped, $1/2$-inch flowers opens over the entire spike, the blossoms collapsing at day's end. Each succeeding day throughout the flowering season, a completely new set of blooms opens.

Pickerel-weed occurs from Prince Edward Island west to Ontario and south to Missouri, Oklahoma, and Florida. With numerous leaf forms and white-flowered forms, it is widely used in water gardens and lily pools as an accent plant.

Common Water-hemlock

Cicuta maculata
Carrot or Parsley Family

Common Water-hemlock is extremely poisonous, especially its 4- to 6-inch long, fleshy, tuberous roots. People have died after eating Common Water-hemlock roots thinking they were wild parsnips. Any plant resembling Queen-Anne's-lace and growing in wet areas, sunny or shady, should be suspect.

The erect stems of Common Water-hemlock are extensively branched and typically purple-spotted, reaching heights of 2 to 6 feet. Throughout the summer the plants produce tiny, 5-petaled white flowers in loose umbels 2 to 8 inches across and typical of the Carrot Family.

A biennial, Common Water-hemlock ranges from Quebec to Manitoba south to Maryland, North Carolina, Tennessee, Missouri, and Texas.

Buttonbush

Cephalanthus occidentalis
Madder Family

One of our most aquatic of shrubs, Buttonbush often grows in the standing waters of permanent ponds and lakeshores where it roots by declining stems and can form tangled thickets. Its large, handsome, glossy green leaves are opposite or whorled on plants that can grow 6 to 7 feet tall in swamps. Flowers occur in clusters of showy, round, ball-like heads with prominent stigmas that give the blossoms a fuzzy appearance. Very attractive to butterflies, bees, and other insects, the flowers bloom throughout July and August.

Buttonbush is widely distributed throughout the western hemisphere and capable of becoming a small tree. All parts of the shrub are poisonous, particularly the roots.

129

fwc

Nodding Beggar-ticks; Stick-tight; Nodding Bur-marigold
Bidens cernuus
Aster or Daisy Family

An autumn walk through dried ponds, marshes, or swales can provide an unwelcome introduction to Nodding Beggar-ticks when its clinging seeds with their barbed awns attach to any clothing they touch. In spite of its pesky fruits, however, this plant produces showy yellow flowers resembling those of coreopsis in late summer and early fall, often in masses that present a wide, golden swath. Erect in bloom but strongly nodding in fruit, the flower heads feature 8 to 10 broad ray flowers surrounding a domed head of orange-yellow disk flowers.

The stems of Nodding Beggar-ticks can be simple or highly branched, ranging in height from several inches to 5 or 6 feet. Leaves are somewhat willow-like and strongly toothed.

Found across most of North America, Nodding Beggar-ticks is often abundant for a year or two on marshes newly exposed as Great Lakes levels drop. Eventually, though, more aggressive grasses, sedges, and weeds replace this early colonizer.

tlm

Common Cat-tail and Narrow-leaved Cat-tail
Typha latifolia and T. angustifolia
Cat-tail Family

Two species of this plant occur natively in the Great Lakes region, of which the Common or Broad-leaved (*T. latifolia*) is more widespread. It occurs not only in Great Lakes shoreline marshes but also in ponds, ditches, and streams as well as on hillside seeps, especially if the latter are disturbed. In our area and throughout the world, this species can be distinguished by its relatively wide leaves (1 to 2 inches).

Narrow-leaved Cat-tail is confined primarily to shoreline waters and ditches surrounding the Great Lakes, occurring only rarely in inland marshes and ponds. Where the two grow together, natural hybrids often form.

The flowers of cat-tails are minute and densely clustered into a dense spike. Persistent into fruit, the female flowers and their subsequent seeds constitute the recognizable cat-tail. Male flowers occur above the female and are temporary, gradually drying and falling apart after pollination. Here again, the two species are easily distin-

guishable. In Common Cat-tail, there is no gap between the male and female flowers. In Narrow-leaved Cat-tail, the gap can be $1/2$ to 1 inch or more.

Both cat-tail species are important sources of wildlife food and absorb nutrients and minerals such as excess sewage from lake water. But they are also difficult to control and capable of rapidly clogging smaller, man-made ponds and crowding out normal vegetation in bogs.

131

Fens are wetlands that develop where the water supply is mineral rich, not sterile of nutrients like that of bogs. At first visit, a fen may seem much like a bog, but there are important differences. Ground water, although its flow may be impeded, usually drains slowly through the fen and onward. Therefore, there is more soil oxygen, and the peaty material derived from the decay of the plant materials decomposes further releasing more nutrituous mineral material. Because of the mineral-rich water supply and the greater decomposition of the organic matter present, fen soils may be blackish, muck-like, and neutral to strongly alkaline as opposed to the typically brownish, peaty, acid soil of bogs.

By definition, fens usually support few or no trees, at least in the early stages of their development. Young fens are dominated by grass-like vegetation, usually sedges and rushes. In the open, wetter parts, often with pools of standing water during wet periods, rather significant sedge mats develop. These open mats form the substrate for a number of showy wetland plants including the calopogon orchids, Bogbean, and bladderworts. These and most other fen plants are not strictly limited to fens but occur in suitable wet bogs or wet beach sands as well. Thus one may find pitcher-plants, sundews, and several orchid species in either bog or fen.

In later stages, shrubs may develop in considerable numbers. This fen stage, in some classifications, may be referred to as a shrub karr (carr). As successional plant changes occur, the open fen consolidates sufficiently in places to support the growth of trees. Such fens become treed fens. In northern parts of the Great Lakes region, treed fens frequently develop a predominantly White Cedar forest cover and are known locally as "cedar swamps."

In calcareous fens, the ground water is rich in dissolved calcium bicarbonates. As algae and microscopic organisms extract carbon dioxide from the bicarbonates, the remaining carbonates form insoluble compounds and separate from the water. Mixing with organic wastes from the life in the water, these compounds become a white, somewhat slippery mass called marl. Marl may be almost white or gray, and deep deposits may form. Such deposits can be much like quick-

fwc

sand or very loosely consolidated peat in presenting to visitors the danger of becoming mired and unable to escape.

Large marl deposits occur around the margins of many northern lakes in limestone districts. They also occur with some frequency in the southern Great Lakes region, not only around lakes but on some of the hillside fen seeps once very common along the great moraines of southern Michigan, northern Indiana, northern Illinois, Wisconsin, and Minnesota. Some calcareous fen waters become so charged with dissolved calcium compounds that the minerals precipitate out onto vegetation in the form of a loosely consolidated limestone rock called tuffa. If such water wells up in a single large spring, it may spread out and precipitate a circular wall or dam. Water then rises higher to surmount the dam, precipitating more lime tuffa as it flows over the dam and raising it even higher. Occasionally this "dam" is so efficient that the height of the spring is gradually raised several feet above the surrounding landscape into a large raised dome with a spring flowing from its top. Such domed fens still occur in some parts of southern Michigan.

Depending upon the richness of the minerals plus other special conditions, a fen may undergo a plant succession that leads to a sphagnum moss lawn and further development from alkaline fen to acid sphagnum moss-peat bog. Others develop into the treed fen cedar swamp with a quite different flora.

Westward in the Great Lakes region, the drier edges of fen lakes or hillside seep fens grade almost imperceptibly into moist or mesic prairie or, in wetter regions, into marsh. Northward fens grade into treed fen-cedar-fir forest, and even farther north, much fen vegetation also invades drier ground.

Small White Lady's-slipper
Cypripedium candidum
Orchid Family

The Small White Lady's-slipper is the most sun-loving of the native lady's-slippers. Classified as rare or endangered in much of the region, it is increasingly threatened by habitat destruction, particularly because it grows in soils that make good muck farms for such crops as celery and onions. This habitat is also a favorite of Massasauga Rattlesnakes, which one frequently encounters on expeditions to see Small White Lady's-slippers.

Despite its localized occurrence, the Small White Lady's-slipper often forms large colonies. Fragrant flowers appear from mid-May into early June on clumps of 6- to 16-inch single-flowered stalks. Each waxy-white, polished, egg-shaped pouch is purple-veined inside and often purple blotched about the opening. Floral companions of the species are Grass Pink, Eastern Prairie Fringed-orchids, and Golden Alexanders, the latter being the best indicator plant for the species.

Small White Lady's-slippers range as far west as Nebraska, the Dakotas, and Manitoba where they will also grow on drier prairie hillsides.

Golden Alexanders
Zizia aurea
Carrot or Parsley Family

Golden Alexanders thrive in numerous habitats across a wide geographical range but are characteristic of open fens, sunny wet meadows, and moist prairies in the southern Great Lakes region. Often red-tinged, plants grow 1 to 1½ feet tall and feature compound leaves up to 8 inches long comprised of leaflets with serrated edges. From April to June, tiny bright yellow flowers are evident in umbrella-like clusters 1 to 1½ inch across.

Emitting a strong parsley odor when crushed and poisonous like some other members of the Carrot Family, Golden Alexanders is every man's best guide to the Small White and Small Yellow Lady's-slippers that bloom at the same time and place.

Three-leaved False Solomon-seal
Smilacina trifolia
Lily Family

A characteristic ground cover in northern treed fens and cedar swamps, Three-leaved False Solomon-seal forms a carpet of silky green leaves that sometimes harbor orchid treasures. Preferring the "soupiest" of wet conditions, it also inhabits cedar and black spruce bogs and sphagnum mats.

Three-leaved False Solomon-seal spreads by underground runners, so what appears to be many plants could be one clone. It bears tiny white flowers (½ inch wide) in few-flowered pyramidal racemes between mid-May and mid-July – one of the earliest plants to bloom after cold temperatures moderate.

137

jrw

Small Yellow Lady's-slipper
Cypripedium parviflorum
Orchid Family

Found primarily in calcareous fens, the Small Yellow Lady's-slipper (var. *makasin*, formerly merged with var. *parviflorum*) is most common in the southern area of our region at the edges of prairie fens and moist depressions in old fields. Unlike its white relative, which often grows nearby, it prefers the light shade under the edges of shrubs such as Gray-twigged Dogwood and willow.

Usually about a foot tall, rarely up to 2 feet tall, it may grow individually or in clumps if conditions are optimal. Flowering occurs in May and June and even into July in cold cedar swamps. Compared with the Large Yellow Lady's-slipper, the blossoms are smaller and more fragrant with maroon spotting around the lip opening. The petals, almost solid maroon-purple, are usually shorter than those of the large yellow slipper and less drooping, carried horizontally, and most frequently quite twisted.

fwc

Large Yellow Lady's-slipper
Cypripedium parviflorum
Orchid Family

The Large Yellow Lady's-slipper (var. *pubescens*) inhabits northern treed fens and upland deciduous or mixed forests in the Great Lakes region, though it ranges widely from eastern Canada south through Georgia and Alabama west to Texas and northwest as far as the Yukon, British Columbia, and Alaska. In our area it particularly favors old fields in limestone districts as well where it often grows in dense beds of Poison Ivy. It may also be found in swamp forests.

Extremely variable in size depending on the genetic strain and growing conditions, the Large Yellow Lady's-slipper produces 1 to 2 flowers per plant in May and June. Its lip is an egg-shaped pouch that is pale to clear yellow outside and variously streaked or spotted with brownish-purple on the inside.

tlm

fwc

Showy Lady's-slipper; Queen's Lady's-slipper
Cypripedium reginae
Orchid Family

This majestic orchid is the largest and showiest of the region's native orchids and the state flower of Minnesota. The most moisture-loving of the lady's-slippers, it prefers wet, open habitats, especially the bright, sunny openings of northern fens. It is most abundant in calcareous areas where it will also invade bare ditch soils.

Showy Lady's-slippers can reach a height of 3 feet and produce up to 3 flowers per stalk from early June to mid-July. Their distinctive coloration can vary greatly, but the pouch-shaped lip is most commonly white with heavy rose-purple streaking. The flat, white, bluntly rounded petal tips differ from those of all our other lady's-slippers. Also characteristic are the conspicuous short hairs on the stem and the backs of the leaves that can cause a contact dermatitis in some people.

Attracted by its rich vanilla-like fragrance, deer sometimes graze heavily on Showy Lady's-slippers. In spite of the damage to individual plants, cedar swamps overbrowsed by deer produce the most magnificent slipper colonies because the deer browsing opens the cover and lets in the light.

141

Star-grass
Hypoxis hirsuta
Amaryllis Family

This diminutive species is the only member of the Amaryllis Family in our region's flora. Difficult to spot when not in bloom, Star-grass leaves can be 6 inches tall but are very narrow and grass-like. Its small, bright yellow flowers appear in clusters of 3 to 9 on stalks up to 4 inches long. Lasting only a few days each, the blooms occur from late April to June and sometimes into August and September.

In the South, this species, oddly enough, may be found in dry woods as well as in wet, open meadows – wherever there is freedom from competition. In some areas, it is often seen in disturbed soil devoid of other vegetation.

Angelica
Angelica atropurpurea
Carrot or Parsley Family

Growing to 10 feet tall, Angelica is likely our largest herbaceous wildflower. Its usually purple, smooth stem bears large compound leaves that sheathe the main stem with their bases and have tooth-edged leaflets 3 to 5 inches long. Spherical clusters of small white flowers appear in June and July followed in late summer by flat, 2-parted smooth fruits that separate at maturity and disperse by wind or water.

Angelica ranges throughout the Great Lakes region south into the mountains of North Carolina.

142

Wood Lily
Lilium philadelphicum
Lily Family

The Wood Lily ranges in varying habitats from the East Coast to Alaska and down the Rockies to Arizona, New Mexico, and Colorado although it is far more abundant in the northeast. The Great Lakes region's only lily with up-ward-facing flowers, it grows in mead-ows, along roadsides, and at the edges of woodlands in northern Michigan as well as in treed fens.

Particularly common in limestone districts, Wood Lily inhabits fens for the soil chemistry, not for the moisture. It flowers from mid-June to mid-August with blossoms up to 4 inches across varying in color from a flat, harsh orange to reds with an occasional citron yellow. Orange-red to pinkish-red are most common. Although usually single-flowered, the 1- to 3-foot plants can bear up to 4 or 5 blooms. Like all true lilies, Wood Lily has whorled leaves, i.e. they occur in multiples at single points around the stem. Those of Wood Lily are finely-toothed at the point of attachment to the stem.

Tiger Swallowtail Butterflies pollinate the fragrant Wood Lily flowers by perching on the tops of open blossoms and grasping the narrow petals with thin legs while sucking the abundant nectar.

fwc

Shrubby Cinquefoil
Potentilla fruticosa
Rose Family

Shrubby Cinquefoil grows worldwide, a bushy-branched shrub of moist, calcareous soil ranging in size from dwarf varieties in the Himalayas to hip-high specimens in the southern Great Lakes region. In this area, its stems often arch and intermingle forming impenetrable, dense thickets 3 to 4 feet high.

The leaves of Shrubby Cinquefoil are 3-lobed and only 1 inch long. From June to October, golden 1-inch flow-

ers dot the branch tips. In the wild, these are usually bright yellow although white, lemon, and orange mutations do occur.

Shrubby Cinquefoil is a good indicator of White Lady's-slippers, Grass Pinks and rattlesnakes in southern fens. Widely regarded for its horticultural value, it is now quite common as a landscape plant though it prefers the cooler northern zones.

Swamp Thistle
Cirsium muticum
Aster or Daisy Family

Swamp Thistle is a prickly biennial that grows in fens, wet thickets, and meadows throughout the region and south into the North Carolina mountains. Although tall, it is one of the more delicate of the group of thistles. In its first year, the plant produces a rosette of leaves up to 10 inches long. The second year brings leafy flowering stalks up to 6 feet tall that bear purplish flower heads from July through September. Borne on stems that can be quite airy, the heads are actually numerous individual flowers surrounded by narrow, leaf-like structures called bracts. In late fall, the flower heads release downy clusters of seeds, each seed having its own white "parachute" that aids in wind dispersal. Small birds, especially wild canaries, use the seed down as nest lining.

145

Tall White Bog-orchid; Bog-Candle
Platanthera dilitata
Orchid Family

Tall White Bog-orchids are also called Fragrant White Bog-orchids because of their spicy odor resembling cloves and Bog-candles in reference to their tall, narrow spikes. The species ranges across North America from the southern Great Lakes northward but now is much less common in the southern Great Lakes due largely to habitat destruction. Only 9 plants are currently documented in Indiana, all at a single northern site. In the Pacific Northwest, however, it can be found by the tens of thousands.

A sun-lover, the Tall White Bog-orchid does not flower in shade. It usually occurs, therefore, as scattered single plants in open areas of fens. The plants typically grow to 2 feet tall, but the flowers are relatively tiny at only about $\frac{1}{2}$ inch long with a spear-head-shaped lip that is dilated near its base. Like several of its relatives, the Tall White Bog-orchid retains its spent flowers after pollination. In late summer, it may display both petals and split seed pods.

Cowbane
Oxypolis rigidor
Carrot or Parsley Family

An inconspicuous plant even when blooming, Cowbane grows at the edges of swamps, marshes, and fens. Reaching heights more than 3 feet tall, its delicate stems feature narrow leaves comprised of narrower leaflets arranged in rows along the mid vein. Each leaflet may have small teeth or smooth margins. Flat-topped, white flower clusters up to 4 inches wide appear in late summer.

Riddell's Goldenrod
Solidago riddellii
Aster or Daisy Family

One of many goldenrods, Riddell's Goldenrod is named for medical botanist John Riddell who lived in the early nineteenth century. Characteristic of open calcareous fens in the southern part of the region, it features leaves that are longitudinally folded where they join the stem. Riddell's Goldenrod produces flat-topped flower clusters comprised of 20 to 30 individual tiny flowers in each head and can form a broad expanse of color in early to midsummer when it blooms. Fluffy white "parachutes" carry its mature seeds away on wind gusts.

147

jrw

fwc

Grass-of-Parnassus
Parnassia glauca
Saxifrage Family

From July to October, given proper moisture levels, Grass-of-Parnassus often grows so abundantly along the Great Lakes shorelines as to form a white stripe as far as the eye can see — a sure indicator of summer's decline. A characteristic plant of southern and particularly northern treed fens, it also can be abundant on wet limestone lakeshores of the Great Lakes, one of several species of the same general appearance that occur in the region. The yellowish, glistening structures in the flowers are considered to be "false nectaries" that function to lure the pollinating insects to the flower but offer no reward.

Heart-shaped, leathery leaves at the base of the plant are usually about 1 inch wide but can be larger. Each leaf cluster produces several flower stalks up to 12 inches high – a very tall stem for such a dense, low cluster of leaves. Single, star-shaped flowers up to 1 inch across appear at the tip of each stalk, opening over a period of several days. Creamy-colored with deep silvery-green veins, the blossoms have a seersucker appearance.

Grass-of-Parnassus is very poisonous if ingested.

Forget-me-not
Myosotis scorpioides
Borage Family

A small, charming blue flower with a yellow center, Forget-me-not occurs in the far north woods of the region, particularly in wetlands, seeps, and ditches near Lake Superior. Preferring a habitat with a bubbly, flowing spring, seepage areas, or even moist roadside ditches, it may form large mats of interconnected plants that grow to 6 inches tall with leaves 2 inches long. From May to September, its flowers uncurl on their stemlets like an uncoiling scorpion's tail, hence its species name.

Forget-me-not is a European import that escaped from early gardens and became naturalized. Its primary pollinators are a unique group of flies that hover over the flowers like hummingbirds while inserting their long tongues to drink nectar. It occurs widely over the northeast south to the Carolinas.

Fringed Gentian
Gentianopsis procera
Gentian Family

The unique blue color and distinctly fringed petals of its flowers make this species easy to identify from mid-August to October. One of two native Fringed Gentians, the plant grows to 1 foot tall and may be single stemmed or multi-branched with pairs of narrow leaves up to 3 inches long. It bears showy 2-inch flowers at the branch tips. In comparison with the acid soil species (*G. crinita*), *G. procera* rarely occurs outside limestone districts or calcareous fens, is a lighter blue color, flowers more sparsely, and has much narrower leaves. Both are biennial, making only leaves the first year and flowering then dying the second year.

Pollinated by bees and preferring open habitats with little competition from other plants, Fringed Gentian is almost impossible to cultivate. It is a protected species in Michigan and deserving of wider protection beyond.

Bogs

dmb

The term "bog" is the subject of varying interpretations and definitions, even among meticulous ecologists. We prefer that of Botanist James Pringel of the Royal Botanic Gardens, Hamilton, Ontario, Canada. According to him, a bog is an essentially undrained, peat-filled wetland with strongly acid, mineral poor soil, supporting on its surface a specialized flora with the soil surface dominated by various species of sphagnum moss.

Bogs occur most frequently in recently glaciated regions, usually in depressions left by ice blocks that melted forming undrained ponds or lakes.

Shallow lakes where sunlight can reach the bottom develop bogs faster than deep lakes because increased available light causes more prolific plant growth with subsequent greater amounts of peat formed.

Bog development starts with growth of submerged aquatic plants. With limited oxygen in the water, the action of decay bacteria is diminished. If the soil (and hence the water) is fertile, plant growth per year exceeds the amount that can completely decay in one season. Plant remains break down partially into a shapeless brownish mass termed peat that settles to the

bottom of the depression. Eventually, deep beds of peat accumulate and reach almost to the surface of the water providing footing for emergent plants – reeds, sedges, grasses – and waterlilies. The partially decomposed roots in the ever-accumulating peat bind it in the shallows and sheltered coves, accelerating the buildup to the surface there, and bog development is on its way! As more exposed peat appears at the surface, first sedge then moss mats appear. Each stage contributes its peat material, finally raising the peat to or above the water surface. These moss mats become invaded by specialized shrubs, often of the Heath family. Bog trees – Black Spruce (*Picea mariana*) and Tamarack – follow the shrubs, appearing first in older, somewhat drier shrub zones.

At this stage, a bog is a fascinating, enchanting, exciting, and potentially dangerous place. In the open water that remains from the original lake, aquatic plants grow in the deepest areas; emergents and now often solid beds of waterlilies thrive adjacent to the shore. But the "shore" is a marginal mat, a buoyant shelf of varying widths of floating moss bound together by the roots and stems of the bog heaths. Such exposed peat and soft sphagnum moss mats provide wet, acidic, competition-free beds that harbor carnivorous plants, native orchids, and other delicate, beautiful flowers, and very large colonies may develop. Because the marginal mat is constantly encroaching upon the pond surface with bog development, there is, for years, always a new section of mat and therefore a new bed for flower development if the bog is not disturbed or drained.

Walking on that mat is a unique experience. As one moves, the ground quivers and shakes, giving the sense of walking on a waterbed. Large trees many feet away shake. A pole thrust into the mat may disappear completely through the peat and into underlying water. It is possible for a visitor to fall through and drown. In the past, prehistoric animals have done so and been preserved for thousands of years. Even well-preserved human remains have been recovered from old peat bogs in

Europe. The strong acids formed in the peat act as a preservative for pollen grains and plant and animal remains and have allowed us to map post-ice age forests and reconstruct the past.

Slowly, bog mats encroach and close over the pond. From an aerial view these pothole bogs appear zoned, much like a bull's eye target, as the stages encroach ever inward. In terms of plant succession, it is like moving backwards in time, with the oldest stages (and flora) near the outer edge and the youngest nearest the center of the lake. Eventually the bog completely covers any open water, and finally the entire former lake surface becomes the bog forest. In any given spot, as one dominant stage succeeds another, the surface plants, the wildflowers, give way to new sets tolerant of the newly developing conditions.

Bogs in the southern Great Lakes region especially may develop a moat or lagg around their outer margins, making them difficult to enter in wet seasons. In the far north of our region,

along oceans, and across northern North America, extensive areas of "patterned fen," another type of peatland with nearly identical surface conditions to our pothole bogs, develop, but their flora is less varied than that of our Great Lakes pothole bogs.

A delicate and easily damaged environment, a bog takes hundreds of years to develop. Present bogs of the Great Lakes region are about 10,000 years old, dating to the retreat of the last glaciers. A bog's assemblage of native plants is a unique feature of our region. Many rare and unusual plants and animals occur only here. Drainage, off-road vehicles, fire, exotic plants, excessive foot-travel – all can disrupt, damage, or destroy a bog.

In the western Great Lakes region occur more outstanding bogs than remain anywhere else in the United States. Regrettably, many have already been damaged or destroyed. It is therefore most expedient to save those we can for the scientific information they yield, their beauty and wonder, their

rare occupants, and the enjoyment of posterity. After all, they will be with us for only a relatively short while longer as the process of succession continues to convert them to solid ground.

Bog-laurel
Kalmia polifolia
Heath Family

Bog-laurel is one of the earliest flowering shrubs to bloom in the northern Great Lakes, turning open bogs into drifts of pink from May into June. A smooth-stemmed, typically straggly shrub, it can grow up to 40 inches tall. Its flowers, bright pink miniatures of the larger white Mountain-laurel, are ³/₄ inch wide and grow from the tips of the stems. Tiny fruits, often glossy dark red, appear above the leaves in late summer.

Bog-laurel has opposite, narrow, evergreen leaves, lustrous green above and white beneath. Many botanists believe its rolled leaf margins help the plant conserve water. This may seem contradictory in a bog habitat, but the acidity of the peat prevents certain plants from absorbing enough water.

One of two native laurels, Bog-laurel does not tolerate shade. Like most laurels, its foliage can be poisonous to humans and livestock as can honey made from some species.

Labrador-tea
Ledum groenlandicum
Heath Family

Pictured with Bog-laurel are the white blossoms of Labrador-tea. A low-growing evergreen shrub of northern bogs and cedar swamps across northeastern North America, Labrador-tea has hairy twigs that bear alternate leaves with rolled edges and brown, woolly undersides. The small white flowers occur in June in clusters up to 3 inches across.

During the revolutionary war, Labrador-tea was used as a substitute for commercial tea, though its product is of dubious quality. Recent chemical studies show that this species may actually better be classified in the genus *Rhododendron* rather than *Ledum*.

154

fwc

Cotton-grass; Bog-cotton
Eriophorum viridi-carinatum
Sedge Family

Cotton-grass belongs to the sedge family, a very large family of native, grass-like plants. The farther north one goes, the more plentiful Cotton-grass becomes in open bogs. Called Alaskan Cotton in our forty-ninth state, it is abundant on the Arctic tundra. It occurs also in colonies in wet, sandy ditches along northern roadsides and in bogs. Plants typically grow 2 feet tall with several smooth, narrow leaves attached to stiffly erect stems topped by one or more clusters of inconspicuous flowers. Its characteristic white cottony appearance results from the production of long, soft bristles in the maturing seed head. This most distinctive feature of the plant likely influenced selection of its Latin genus name *Eriophorum* which means "to bear wool or cotton." The white "cotton" develops in spring or early summer and persists long into the following winter.

fwc

Buckbean; Bogbean
Menyanthes trifoliata
Buckbean Family (formerly
Gentian Family)

This semi-aquatic, low-growing perennial grows in bogs, ponds and tundra pools in colder regions throughout the northern hemisphere. In the southern Great Lakes region, it occurs only in colder bogs, bog ponds, and quagmires. White, hair-like projections on its petals give a beautiful frosted look to the terminal flower clusters. Its creeping submerged rhizome bears thickish flower stems. Leaves arise from the rhizome or flower stem, each leaf bearing 3 leaflets up to 6 inches long and 2 inches wide. Flowers appear in spring in the south of our region, usually in late May or early June farther north. In Europe, Buckbean root is used as an aid to digestion, though its value and safety in this regard are unknown.

Wild Calla; Water-arum
Calla palustris
Arum Family

Wild Calla, a native perennial herb that sometimes forms very large colonies from its branched, creeping rhizomes, grows locally in cool woodland bogs and ponds across northern North America. It blooms heavily in spring, but occasional flowers appear throughout the growing season. The alternate leaves arise from the underwater rhizome and expand abruptly into a heart-shaped, silky-smooth, blade-like leaf up to 15 inches long. The white petal-like spathe, a modified leaf resembling a petal, attracts pollinators to the cluster of inconspicuous flowers it surrounds.

Wild Calla is a member of the Jack-in-the-Pulpit family. Biting into Wild Calla will cause a burning sensation in the mouth due to the presence of calcium oxalate crystals characteristic of many members of that family.

fwc

Arethusa; Dragon's Mouth
Arethusa bulbosa
Orchid Family

Arethusa, one of the area's most beautiful native orchids, ranges primarily throughout northeastern North America. Its arched sepals and large lip suggest an animal's face. Botanists Morris and Eames described their first encounter with Arethusa in a sphagnum bog as follows: "The feeling was irresistible that we had surprised some strange sentient creature in its secret bower of moss; that it was alert and listening intently with pricked up ears."

Considered rare, Arethusa has become so from bog destruction at the south of its range but may still be encountered frequently in more northern regions.

This small orchid, rarely more than 8 inches tall, bears its single 1- to 2-inch flower on a smooth, slender scape. A single grass-like leaf at the base of the flowering stalk is scarcely evident until after flowering. The fleshy, food-storing bulb, anchored loosely in the moss, is easily destroyed by picking. White and bright orchid-pink flower forms occur from early June to mid-July, the pink being most frequent.

fwc

**Northern Pitcher-plant,
Huntsman's-Cup, Sidesaddle
Flower**
Sarracenia purpurea
Pitcherplant Family

Leaves of the Northern Pitcher-plants are among the most uniquely constructed of any plant. Solid red, solid green (in shade) or green with red veins, the leaves form a pitcher-like cavity with a hood on one side and a wing on the other. Glands on the hood, pitcher-rim, and wing secrete a chemical attractant that also contains a muscle relaxant and a narcotic. As a hapless insect feeds, it slowly loses muscle control and falls into the rain-filled passive trap. Its attempts to crawl from the trap are thwarted by downward-pointing hairs lining the inside of the hood as well as by the slippery

rolled rim. Unable to get a grip, the insect eventually falls into the water below. Wetting agents secreted into the water by the leaf cause the prey to sink to the trap bottom where protein-digesting enzymes (in some species at least) directly digest the insect. In this water-filled species, some scientists suspect that microorganisms present in the water aid in decomposing the prey.

Although the Pitcher-plant's evergreen leaves are quite showy, the plant is most conspicuous in late May and early June when it displays rich maroon, or rarely clear yellow, solitary

158

fwc

flowers. It may be found in bogs across the entire northern sector of North America as far west as British Columbia. The official flower of the Province of Newfoundland and Labrador where it appears on one of their coins, this and several other pitcher-plants also occur in the southeastern United States.

fwc

159

fwc

Rose Pogonia
Pogonia ophioglossoides
Orchid Family

Usually less than 1 foot tall, Rose Pogonia exhibits considerable variation in color, from pure white to deep pink with rose being typical. It also possesses a distinct fragrance that philosopher Henry David Thoreau compared to the odor of garter snakes, but the smell is most often associated with that of red raspberries and can sometimes be detected before one encounters the plants.

Native in the eastern half of North America from Texas to Newfoundland and westward through Minnesota in the Great Lakes region, it grows in the wettest sunny bogs, swamps, and fens.

One of the few orchids to multiply from root runners as well as from seed, Rose Pogonia forms dense colonies. It flowers in June and July, but a given colony does not always bloom heavily every year.

Grass-pink

Calopogon tuberosus
Orchid Family

One of the most familiar Great Lakes orchids, Grass-pink occurs from Newfoundland and the subarctic all the way south to Cuba but becomes increasingly scarce near civilization. Occasionally found on moist prairies, it most commonly grows, in our region, in open glades in sphagnum bogs and fens.

Grass-pink attracts bees with its brilliant magenta color but deceives them by offering no nectar reward. Its lip, borne uppermost unlike most orchids, is hinged near its base and bears stalked, enlarged yellow hairs appearing falsely as pollen grains. When a bee lands, its weight causes the lip hinge to release, plopping the bee forcibly against the stigma. If the bee is carrying pollen, the pollen lands upon the stigma pollinating the flower. In its struggle to get away, the bee picks up new pollen and carries it to the next flower.

This native orchid produces a wiry, slender scape up to 18 inches tall from a starchy corm. The scape bears a raceme of several showy 2-inch flowers from late June until early August in our range. Like Arethusa, it bears a single grass-like leaf arising from its base and sheathing the flower stem. Later in the season, pollinated flowers produce 1-inch cylindrical green seed pods.

161

fwc

jrw

Horned Bladderwort
Utricularia cornuta
Bladderwort Family

Horned Bladderworts grow in colonies of many individual flowering stems, carpeting peat mats and beach flats throughout the western Great Lakes region. The snap-dragon-like flowers have a spur projecting from the bottom and are pollinated by bees. Like sundews and pitcherplants, the carnivorous bladderworts trap and digest prey. They feed upon microscopic protozoa and tiny creatures in the mud or pondwater in which they live. Unlike the floating bladderworts (see bladderworts in *Ponds and Marshes*), the traps of Horned Bladderwort lie buried in sand, mud, or peat and perhaps are not as functional as those of the free-floating species.

This showy native blooms heavily from late June until August, each 6- to 10-inch stem displaying 1 to several large yellow flowers at a time.

Round-leaved Sundew
Drosera rotundifolia
Sundew Family

Spatulate-leaved Sundew
Drosera intermedia
Sundew Family

Tiny members of a vast worldwide family, sundews are unable to acquire enough nutrients from their bog habitat to prosper. To obtain needed nourishment they have developed a carnivorous habit. The small leaves widen at the tips into traps capable of catching and digesting insects. The leaf hairs secrete a sticky fluid. The brighter the sunlight, the more fluid the plant produces, hence the common name Sundew. Insects attracted to the plant for food become entangled in this viscous substance and cannot escape. The movable, protein-sensitive hairs center the prey on the leaf, then the leaf curls about the victim. Enzymes secreted by the leaf digest the insect and the plant absorbs the digested nutrients. Afterwards, the leaf reopens and pushes the insect carcass to its edge.

These delicate plants produce small circular rosettes of several leaves, generally maroon red, that may be over 2 inches long individually. The very small white flowers emerge on slender scapes that arise from the center of each rosette. Single 1/3- to 1/2-inch flowers open one at a time over a period of several weeks, resulting ultimately in a 3- to 8-inch bloom stalk that appears to uncoil.

Round-leaved Sundew grows worldwide in the northern hemisphere. Spatulate-leaved Sundew ranges throughout the eastern U.S. at the edges of ponds and ditches and in bogs, almost always in bright sun and the wettest places. It is, in fact, a good indicator of places NOT to walk as it grows in the most treacherous spots at the edge of the bog mat.

Several rarer species of sundews also occur in the region, mostly in limestone fens along upper Great Lakes shorelines.

163

tlm

fwc

White Fringed-orchid
Platanthera blephariglottis
Orchid Family

The sun-loving White Fringed-orchid grows more commonly in the Great Lakes region than does the similarly structured Yellow Fringed-orchid, inhabiting open glades or sphagnum mats of peat bogs almost exclusively here. Although not very common, it can be locally abundant. The White Fringed-orchid ranges from Texas to Newfoundland and westward in the north to southern Ontario and Lower Michigan. It has not reached Michigan's Upper Peninsula or Wisconsin but exists very locally in southern Illinois, on the Cumberland Plateau, and in one or two bogs in eastern Ohio. Although it grows in southwestern Michigan very near the state border, it has never been found in Indiana. Blooming in July and early August, the White-fringed Orchid often occurs with the Yellow Fringed-orchid, giving rise to buff- and lemon-colored hybrids.

fwc

Yellow Fringed-orchid
Platanthera ciliaris
Orchid Family

The Yellow Fringed-orchid, with its bright yellow to orange color, is one of the most brilliant of our native orchids. It grows primarily in the south where it can be found in almost any acid soil, wet or dry, in sunny locations. In the north it is confined to wet sands and peat bogs, perhaps because their soils do not freeze deeply. Southern Lower Michigan is the northwestern limit of its very wide range that extends from Massachusetts through Illinois and Arkansas into Texas.

Rare and protected in the Great Lakes area, the Yellow Fringed-orchid often forms large colonies of plants 18 to 30 inches tall that flower in late July and August. Like the White Fringed-orchid, it has a central tongue-like lip with fringe on the edge. At the back of the lip is a hole extending into a tubular spur containing nectar. Pollinating insects, often butterflies and moths, land on the lip and probe the spur, at the same time inadvertently picking up pollen to be carried to the next flower.

Common Cranberry; Large Cranberry
Vaccinium macrocarpon
Heath Family

Common Cranberry, native only to northeastern North America, grows in bogs and wet sands from Minnesota to Newfoundland south through the Great Lakes States and along the mountains to West Virginia and North Carolina. First used by the Indians for commerce, cranberries are now a major industry in Wisconsin, New Jersey and New England.

Cranberry flowers appear in June and July and look like miniature Shooting Star blossoms. The berries don't turn red until very late in the season. Because they are tasteless and mushy if frozen before they ripen and because they lack sales appeal unless bright red, growers often flood cranberry bogs at night in late fall to prevent their freezing and drain them during the day to allow the berries to ripen and color. In wild situations, the frozen berries remain on the plant through the winter until eaten by wildlife.

Poison Sumac
Toxicodendron vernix
Cashew Family

Poison Sumac, for many, is the most poisonous native contact plant in the Great Lakes region causing, for some, an itchy rash worse than that of the related Poison Ivy. Strictly a wetlands plant of bogs and fens and common here only in the southern half of the region, it ranges across eastern North America south to the Gulf of Mexico. This stout-stemmed, clump-forming shrub has branches with steel gray bark, few or no small twigs, and dangling smooth white berries. Its compound leaves cluster at the ends of branches, reminiscent of a feather duster, and have red petioles. In the fall this shrub can be the most brilliant scarlet of any native shrub prompting many people to pick it for decoration and thereafter suffer the consequences. None of the *red-berried* sumacs, however, are poisonous to touch. In fact, boiled juice of the red-berried forms makes a tasty "lemonade."

Highbush Blueberry
Vaccinium corymbosum
Heath Family

A parent of commercial blueberries, Highbush Blueberry grows natively in acid soil regions of most of the eastern United States from the southern Appalachians north to New England and central Michigan. In our region it grows predominantly in bogs where it displays a beautiful soft-red fall foliage. With rough-bark and multistems, the shrub grows in 5- to 10- foot clumps with narrow, alternate deciduous leaves 1 to 3 inches long. In May and June it bears clusters of small, urn-shaped flowers resembling those of Lily-of-the-Valley in general appearance and having united petals of creamy white. Glaucous blue delicious fruits ripen in August. Often more flavorful than commercial berries, they provide sweet eating both for humans and wildlife.

167

The term "prairie" conjures up a picture of vast, treeless, rolling plains such as those of central North America. Grasses dominate this landscape, becoming increasingly shorter and more sparse as one moves westward and the rainfall drops well below 25 inches per year. However, in the central and eastern reaches of this prairie life zone are much less extensive areas where water is not so limited. These areas we have included as wet meadows and mesic prairies. While grasses and sedges may dominate in these habitats, one also finds a number of more showy broad-leaved herbs that are unique to rich soil, moderate rainfall, and strong sunlight.

In much of our coverage area, true prairie is a successional stage, not permanent, and therefore requires some form of disturbance, natural or otherwise, to maintain it. Such disturbances could be repeated fires and/or periodic water table fluctuations that kill the trees that would ultimately succeed the prairie grasses, herbs, and shrubs. Along with some typical prairie plants, the wetter Great Lakes prairie habitats feature a strange mixture of meadow, marsh, and floodplain plants with a smattering of true prairie species that have reached the area by some chance event.

Moist prairie exists where a high water table is more or less permanent as the result of an underground condition (a clay basin or an impervious substrate that traps water near the surface) or proximity to the Great Lakes.

Found along portions of Lakes Erie, St. Clair, and Huron as well as southern Lake Michigan in Indiana and Illinois, it depends on periods of high and low lake levels for maintenance more than other prairie types in which fire plays a greater role in controlling vegetation. During periods of high water levels, the rising water kills or severely impairs tree growth. As the water level drops in dry years exposing shoreline, bare soil becomes available where prairie plants can develop. Should the lakes remain at a stable level for a number of years, the drier edges of the lake plain prairies will quickly develop a covering of shrubs, primarily Red Twig Dogwood (*Cornus stolonifera*), Silky Dogwood (*Cornus amomum*), Shrubby Cinquefoil, and willows. If the water

level doesn't rise and kill them, restarting the cycle, these shrubs will eventually form a dense cover called "karr."

Lake plain prairie merges imperceptibly into marsh on its wet side and upland or wet meadow on its dry, inland side. Some lake plain species, like Eastern Prairie Fringed-orchid and Blazing-star, are largely confined to this habitat or may occur only very locally elsewhere; others occur in a variety of habitats.

One of the region's most severely endangered habitats, lake plain prairie is now very rare. With soil consisting of rich silt deposits from the water mixed with decaying plant matter, it makes very productive farmland if drained. Close proximity of these prairies to the markets of large Great Lakes

port cities offers further commercial advantage, and more than 90 percent of this prairie has been drained, diked, or ditched for growing cabbages, onions, melons, and grains.

Pockets of moist prairie also occur away from the Great Lakes shores. Called mesic prairie when not on a lake plain, these pockets often include true prairie plants laced with those of calcareous fens and bogs.

Wet meadow is any open moist clearing whether inland or along the shores. Depending on its size and location within the region, it may or may not contain prairie plants. As a general rule, one must go further west to find an abundance of the showy, sun-loving prairie wildflowers. Canada Anemone, New England Aster, Flat-

topped Aster, Bull Thistle, Fireweed, fleabanes, Bottle and Fringed Gentians, Black-eyed Susan, goldenrods and Ironweed dominate wet meadowlands in our region.

The plants presented in this chapter are not grouped by their occurrence in wet meadow, mesic or lake plain prairie. Rather they follow a rough chronological order of blooming time as in previous chapters.

fwc

Shooting-star
Dodecatheon meadia
Primrose Family

A beautiful wildflower with re-flexed petals in colors from white to pink and shades of lilac, Shooting-star is a relative of the European Cyclamen. Thrust forward like a birdbeak, its sta-mens and pistils are dark in contrast to the petals. The largest plants may reach heights of 18 inches, and the roots of this species have a somewhat distinct, pungent, spicy odor reminiscent of licorice. The basal leaves are up to 8 inches long, ovate, and somewhat fleshy near the midrib.

In the western Great Lakes region, Shooting-star is primarily a plant of moist, wet, and mesic prairies although some races of this species grow in woodlands, especially on well-lighted, dripping limestone or sandstone cliffs. It occurs from Pennsylvania into the southwest lower and upper peninsulas of Michigan, Wisconsin, and southern Illinois south to Georgia and Alabama and west as far as Arkansas and Texas.

Prairie Phlox
Phlox pilosa
Phlox Family

Prairie phlox is a variable species with both woodland and prairie races. Its 1 to several erect stems extend up to 2 feet from a basal leaf tuft, producing showy clusters of pink to lavendar flowers from May through July. Often cultivated though sometimes difficult to transplant, Prairie Phlox appropriately carries the species name *pilosa* referring to the short hairs on its leaves and stems. In winter, the stems die back to a woody crown that produces the next year's growth.

Often found associated with such species as White Lady's-slippers and Hoary Puccoon, in our area Prairie Phlox prefers open sandy road banks and dry borders of mesic prairie, often forming large colorful patches.

173

Hoary Puccoon
Lithospermum canescens
Borage Family

Litho means rock and *-spermum* means seed. As its Latin name denotes, this species has hard, stony seeds. But it is most distinguishable by the very fine hairs on its stem and lower leaf surfaces as well as showy orange-yellow flowers. In May and June the trumpet-shaped flowers occur in linear groups that unfurl a little at a time like an uncoiling scorpion's tail. After the flowers fall, fruits (nutlets) develop in the remaining sepal cup.

Hoary Puccoon commonly has thickened red roots and can form dense clumps. Found from Saskatchewan and Ontario south to Georgia and Texas, it occurs in the moister edges of dry sand prairies and the drier edges of prairie fens in the Great Lakes region.

White or Prairie False Indigo
Baptisia lactea
Pea Family

This species of the legume family is on the list of threatened plants in Michigan but may be quite common further west in a range that extends throughout the Great Lakes States south to Texas and north to southwest Ontario. Named False Indigo because indigo dye is sometimes derived from a related species, it occurs in prairies and open woods.

Distinguishable from similar species by its smooth stems and denser spikes of flowers, White False Indigo blooms from May to July with large, bean- or sweet-pea-like flowers in a lupine-like spike. Also recognizable are its 3-parted leaves that turn black upon drying.

174

Eastern Prairie Fringed-orchid

Platanthera leucophaea
Orchid Family

Eastern Prairie Fringed-orchid is the tallest fringed-orchid in our area. A plant of lake plain prairie and drier marsh edges, a habitat now largely destroyed for crop cultivation, Eastern Prairie Fringed-orchid also occurs on sedge mats surrounding bog lakes and, especially eastward, in marl fens. Its distinctive flowers, predominantly white though sometimes greenish to cream, bloom from June to August. Up to an inch wide, individual flowers possess a deeply-fringed, 3-parted lip and overarching, wedge shaped, slightly toothed petals. Their delicious fragrance attracts moth pollinators.

One of the most endangered of our wildflowers, it is native very locally from Maine across the lower Great Lakes States to the Mississippi River. Although formerly locally abundant, it is now a U.S. threatened species. Local numbers fluctuate heavily with changes in Great Lakes water levels.

Foxglove Beard-tongue

Penstemon digitalis
Snapdragon Family

Often found in massive colonies, Foxglove Beard-tongue is conspicuous during its late June flowering peak. Flowering stems 2 to 3 feet high with smooth, lance-shaped leaves extend from a basal rosette of purplish leaves and produce clusters of 1-inch white or purplish-tinged funnel-shaped flowers.

Foxglove Beard-tongue grows from Maine across to South Dakota and southern Quebec south to Virginia, Alabama, Louisiana, and Texas.

175

Spiderwort
Tradescantia ohiensis
Spiderwort Family

Spiderwort grows principally in the southern and western portion of our region where it can occupy a variety of habitats including railroad beds, roadsides, meadows, woodland clearings, and thickets. A plant of full sun, Spiderwort produces stems 1 to 3 feet tall with firm, keeled, narrow, arching leaves up to 1 foot long. It blooms over a long period in the summer from tight bud clusters. The individual showy flowers in purple, rose, or blue last only a day, then hang to one side of the cluster.

Spiderwort ranges throughout much of the eastern United States and is widely cultivated as a garden plant.

Hedge Bindweed
Calystegia sepium
Morning-glory Family

A relative of the morning-glory and similar in appearance, this twining vine has various leaf forms ranging from heart- to arrowhead-shaped. Its large funnel-shaped flowers are white, pink, or a combination of the two.

Frequent on moist prairie and in meadows and ditches, Hedge Bindweed occurs across most of the United States in a number of named varieties.

fwc

Purple Milkweed
Asclepias purpurescens
Milkweed Family

This denizen of damp open woods, savannas, prairies, and moist meadows produces lavender-pink to striking reddish-purple heads of flowers in late June and July in the western Great Lakes region. Individual plants may reach 2 to 4 feet, but unlike Common Milkweed, Purple Milkweed does not form large colonies by means of runners, growing instead as 1- to 3-stemmed plants. Also unlike Common Milkweed, it produces only 1 to 3 clus-

ters of heads at the top of the stem rather than up and down the stem. Like numerous related species, though, it does have milky sap.

Purple Milkweed has recently become quite rare in the northeastern parts of its large range which extends from New England to South Dakota, Oklahoma, and Arkansas as well as south to Tennessee and North Carolina.

177

Queen-of-the-prairie
Filipendula rubra
Rose Family

One of the showy species of wet meadows and prairies, this early summer beauty forms deep rose buds that open into heads of feathery pink plumes. Its compound leaf is somewhat reminiscent of a very large cinquefoil. With thick, running, underground stems, it can form large colonies.

Queen-of-the-prairie ranges from Pennsylvania to Iowa south to Georgia, Kentucky, and Illinois but is quite rare in the eastern part of the Great Lakes region. Although the native form is rare and local in our region, cultivated forms have long been popular with gardeners.

178

Common Marsh-pink; Rose-pink; Rose Gentian
Sabatia angularis
Gentian Family

Common Marsh-pink is a biennial relative of the gentians although it does not resemble a gentian in general appearance. In the first year it produces only a basal rosette of leaves followed the second year by an angular, often branched stem with opposite leaves that grows up to 30 inches tall. Fragrant rose-pink flowers with yellow centers appear at the stem tips from July to September. The 5 petals of each flower are united into a single tube that flares open during the day, revealing the yellow of the petal bases as a star in the center, and closes at night.

Found in moist meadows, prairies, and open acid wood clearings, Common Marsh-pink occurs from Florida across to Louisana and north to the Great Lakes and Ontario where it is rare or local.

Common Fleabane
Erigeron philadelphicus
Aster or Daisy Family

A single fleabane "blossom" with pink petals and a yellow center actually consists of hundreds of yellow disk flowers surrounded by as many as 100 pinkish-white ray flowers to form a "composite" flower, hence its Latin family name (Compositae). With so many seed-producing organs, a single plant can produce a substantial population.

Found in rich thickets and on shores and moist, springy slopes, Common Fleabane is also frequently a weed in gardens. From its basal rosette of oblong leaves, sometimes toothed, grow stems up to 3 feet tall with rounded, almost clasping leaves. Flower heads, nodding and pearl-like in bud, number a few to many per stem.

Common Fleabane ranges across North America in the north and south to Florida and Texas.

179

Fireweed; Great Willow-herb
Epilobium angustifolium
Evening-primrose Family

Disturbed ground is the favorite habitat of this species, particularly following fire. In Great Britain during World War II, Fireweed reappeared on some bombed-out sites after being absent for almost a century. In the Great Lakes it is a plant of sandbars, gravel deposits, burns, disturbed soils, and roadsides where it often forms large and very colorful colonies.

Throughout mid- to late summer, the plants produce flowers on elongated spikes up to 6 feet tall. The rose to purple, or rarely white, 4-petaled flowers open successively from the bottom of the spike upward over a period of several weeks. Its somewhat cylindrical seed capsules split releasing microscopic seeds carried on cottony tufts that serve as parachutes.

Particularly abundant in subarctic regions, Fireweed ranges across North America.

Purple Milkwort
Polygala sanguinea
Milkwort Family

Purple Milkwort grows in damp, raw, acid soils such as may be found in acid sands, the bottoms of old gravel pits, and retreating marshlands. Reaching heights up to 1 foot with linear leaves, this annual can be single-stemmed or feature a bushy branch from a single base. Its pink-lavendar flowers, miniatures of the Fringed Polygala, overlap tightly forming dense clusters at the tops of the stem from summer into fall. Like all polygala flowers, they have 2 "wings" that are petal-like sepals.

Sometimes found in sizable colonies, Purple Milkwort ranges from Nova Scotia to Ontario and southward to South Carolina, Tennessee, Louisiana, and Oklahoma. Contrary to what the name milkwort implies, eating this herb does not cause increased lactation.

180

Hairy Ruellia
Ruellia humilis
Acanthus Family

Hairy Ruellia is a highly variable species that gets its common name from the hairy surfaces of its stem, leaf backs, and leaf margins. The stems can be simple or branched, attaining heights up to 2 feet though branches are reclining to horizontal. Flowers occur in leaf axils and at the top of the stem. Lavendar to bluish, rarely white, petals are united at their bases into a long tube that expands into a funnel shape then ultimately flares widely at the top. Mature fruits of this plant explosively discharge seeds up to 18 feet away.

Hairy Ruellia is native and rare in the extreme south of our area and ranges widely southward and westward.

Culver's-root
Veronicastrum virginicum
Snapdragon Family

Candelabras of elongate, curved flower spikes characterize this tall perennial beauty of calcareous soils. Reaching heights up to 6 feet, Culver's Root possesses sharply toothed, lanceolate, pointed leaves in whorls of 3 to 7. With numerous white or pinkish flowers, it is quite conspicuous when blooming in mid- to late summer.

Local here and more common southward and westward, Culver's Root ranges from Massachusetts and Vermont to Manitoba and south to Florida, Louisiana, and Texas.

fwc

Bull Thistle
Cirsium vulgare
Aster or Daisy Family

With its spiny stem bearing longitudinal, wing-like ridges, this invader of open areas blooms throughout the summer but is distinctive even when not in bloom. A monocarpic species, meaning it flowers once and dies, Bull Thistle typically bears only a set of prickly leaves in its first year. If the plant accumulates enough food during that first year, it flowers, sets seeds, and dies in the second year, making it also a biennial. What appears as a single purple-pink flower head is actually a cluster of many flowers, each capable of producing a single seed. Since one plant can produce many heads, its vast seed production makes Bull Thistle very aggressive.

Introduced from Europe, this widespread weed occurs from Newfoundland to British Columbia southward.

Blazing-star
Liatris spicata
Aster or Daisy Family

In August and September, Blazing-star produces tall, rarely branched spikes of rose-purple flowers. The dense cylinder of composite heads, sometimes 2 feet long, open from the top down on stems up to 4 or 5 feet tall.

Blazing-star requires several years from seed to flowering. A bulbous rhizome (underground stem) must first develop from which the stems arise bearing linear leaves. As with all *Liatris*

plants, the bulb-like rhizome of Blazing-star remains shallowly buried.

Characteristic of mesic prairie and prairie fen borders in the Great Lakes region, this species ranges from Ontario to Minnesota and south to the Gulf Coast. Although blazing-stars are now available from nurseries as a garden plant, this is not the species commonly used for cultivation.

Downy Sunflower
Helianthus mollis
Aster or Daisy Family

This sunflower reaches heights up to 4 feet with distinctive hairy stems and leaves. The "downy" in its common name reflects the velvet-like appearance caused by the whitish hairs. Each stem bears several short-stalked, showy yellow flowers that bloom from August to October. Large colonies may form from spreading underground rhizomes.

For unknown reasons, Downy Sunflower has become extremely rare and often is treated as an endangered species. Perhaps its habitat has become so fragmented as to isolate the plants leading to inbreeding and some loss of adaptability. Individual plants being self-sterile, 2 genetically different plants are required for seed production.

Cutleaf Coneflower
Rudbeckia laciniata
Aster or Daisy Family

Deeply cut, narrowly ovate leaves on a plant up to 9 feet tall make this species easy to identify. Lower leaves are pinnate with 5 to 7 leaflets and attach to the smooth stem with a stalk (petiole). Upper leaves attach directly to the stem and often are 3- to 5-parted. Flowers occur from July to September with weakly spreading yellow petals that droop slightly. The almost spherical, globular, greenish disk at the flower's center becomes columnar in fruit.

Cutleaf-coneflower ranges widely throughout the United States. In our area, it favors the heavier soil of riverbanks, floodplains, woodland borders, and wet meadows. The garden flower Golden-glow is a mutant of this plant with all the disk flowers converted to ray flowers.

Prairie Coneflower; Yellow Coneflower
Ratibida pinnata
Aster or Daisy Family

Prairie Coneflower is one of the most commonly photographed species of prairie landscapes. Tall and rangy in nature, it produces several stems from 1 crown with leaves pinnately divided into 3 to 7 lance-shaped leaflets. In mid- to late summer when in bloom, Prairie Coneflower is particularly conspicuous along roadsides. Like all coneflowers, it produces a small number of ray flowers and numerous disk flowers. The slightly spreading and drooping ray flowers are yellow while the disk flowers form a distinctly dark purple column in the center from which the coneflower name derives.

Found primarily in the southern Great Lakes region, Prairie Coneflower grows from New York across to Nebraska and south to Georgia and Oklahoma.

False Dragonhead; Obedient Plant

Physostegia virginiana
Mint Family

Prized by gardeners and florists because its flower stalks will hold their position when twisted and bent into artistic configurations – hence the name Obedient Plant – this perennial can be 2 to 5 feet tall. Its rather stiffly erect stems are often branched near the top and occur both singly and in clumps.

False Dragonhead blooms from June to September with lavender, pink, or occasionally white flowers. Its united petals form a tube with a lower lip and a hooded upper lip, giving it an appearance vaguely suggestive of snapdragon. The flowers are somewhat ranked one above the other around the stem, appearing from above like 4 vertical rows.

This striking perennial usually prefers the heavier soils of low grounds and river flood plains or lake plain prairies and marshes. Found from southern Quebec to Minnesota and south to New England, Maryland, Tennessee, and Missouri, False Dragonhead is native in the south and central parts of our region. Occurrences in waste areas and meadows in northern Great Lakes stations, however, most likely represent garden escapes.

Canada Tick-trefoil; Beggar's-tick
Desmodium canadense
Pea Family

This showy beggar's-tick occurs in sandier areas of moist prairie, open savanna, and woods. The plant is tall, often 3 to 4 feet, with several somewhat stiff, almost woody herbaceous stems. Flowering racemes occur both in leaf axils along the stem and at the top of the stem. The lavender or pale purple sweet pea-like flowers of this species are relatively showy. A dorsal banner petal bears a dark-margined spot on each side of the mid-vein that is the most conspicuous part of the flower. Later in the season, the seed pod, termed a loment, consists of 5 or 6 large

seeds with the ripe pod so constricted between each that it breaks between seeds on contact with animal hair or human clothing. The hairy seed coats, acting somewhat like "velcro," adhere to the surfaces they contact and are distributed as "ticks" or burrs. Various tick-trefoils can be real pests to woodsmen, hunters, or their dogs.

Canada Tick-trefoil ranges from Nova Scotia to Saskatchewan south to Virginia, Ohio, Missouri, and Oklahoma. Besides Canada Tick-trefoil, there are numerous other species.

187

Common Sneezeweed
Helenium autumnale
Aster or Daisy Family

This intensely yellow daisy of moist meadows and prairies is common on lake plain prairie in our region. Displaying an almost orange tone, its ray flowers are somewhat wedge-shaped with their blunt ends. This attribute combined with stems that bear wings at their corners makes these plants distinctive. Also notable is the sticky resin on the stems.

Found from New England to Minnesota and south to North Carolina and Missouri, this species apparently derives its common name from its bitter, aromatic odor that causes sneezing in some people.

Flat-topped Aster
Aster umbellatus
Aster or Daisy Family

The derivation of the common name of this particular aster is very evident when the plants bloom in September and October. Flowering branches arise from horizontal stems of the previous year and appear to be trimmed to a uniform height. Somewhat larger than those of other common asters, the flowers of this species feature yellow disk flowers and white rays, a combination that gives an impression of creamy white.

Flat-topped Asters occur in Canada from Newfoundland across Ontario and Alberta. In the States, they grow as far south as Kentucky, North Carolina, and Georgia.

Prairie Rosin-weed
Silphium integrifolium
Aster or Daisy Family

Prairie Rosin-weed is a coarse, tall perennial found in the southern and western extremes of our area. Stems up to 6 feet tall feature opposite, smooth-margined leaves and abundant resinous juice. From late July until frost, clusters of large yellow flower heads crown the branch tips with all flowers of each head producing seeds. A plant of sedge meadows, damp ground at the edges of woods, and wet prairies, Prairie Rosin-weed occupies such habitats from Michigan to Kansas, Indiana, and Missouri. The name Rosin-weed derives from the copious resinous juices of the stem in this and other silphiums.

189

Ironweed; Missouri Ironweed
Vernonia missurica
Aster or Daisy Family

Ironweed is one of the handsomest of the large, fall-blooming composites. Reaching heights of 3 to 4 feet, it produces shaggy, button-like flowers in a brilliant purple color from late July to September.

Found from southern Ontario to Iowa south to Alabama, Mississippi, Oklahoma, and Texas, Ironweed is a plant of moist sandy ground, mesic prairie, and low wet meadows.

Meadow-beauty; Deergrass
Rhexia virginica
Melastoma Family

Meadow-beauty is a short-lived perennial found primarily on the southern coastal plain. In the Great Lakes region, southern Lower Michigan is the general northern extent of its range, but local colonies occur in Upper Michigan and Ontario east of Georgian Bay. A plant of sterile or wet acid soils, it fares poorly with competition.

The stems of Meadow-beauty arise from small, white, overwintering tuberous roots to a height of 1 to 3 feet. Four-angled and slightly bristly to the touch, the stems have wings extending lengthwise along them. July and August bring outward-facing buds and flowers in a brilliant deep pink. Bulbous at their base, the flowers narrow at the neck below a 4-cornered opening from which the floral organs emerge—4 slightly irregular, large petals, a series of stamens of varying lengths, and 1 long pistil.

New England Aster
Aster novae-angliae
Aster or Daisy Family

Perhaps our largest and showiest native aster, New England Aster prefers damp thickets, woodlands, and clearings and is a familiar plant of roadside ditches, moist meadows, and abandoned fields. With tall, tough stems that are stiffer and stronger than those of most other native asters, it has leaves tightly grouped near the top of the stem and covered with tiny hairs. At flowering, the lower leaves and stems often dry up and fall giving the plant base a naked appearance.

New England Aster is a late bloomer, coming into its own in September and October as the goldenrods begin to fade. Produced on stalks characterized by resinous dots, flowers are typically purple and yellow though various shades of pink also occur.

Wide-ranging, this species grows from New England across Canada to Quebec and Alberta and south as far as Colorado, Kansas, and Kentucky.

191

Rattlesnake-master
Eryngium yuccifolium
Carrot or Parsley Family

Nothing else in our native flora is quite like Rattlesnake-master. At a distance its sword-like leaves resemble the yucca, a likeness reflected in its species name. Bluish-green with a waxy bloom on their surface, the leaves also have soft teeth or spines. From its cluster of basal leaves, a flower spike grows 3 or more feet tall, branching at the top and bearing dense, ball-like clusters of white flowers in late summer.

Rattlesnake-master is very rare, even threatened, in the eastern part of our region. Further west it is common on moist prairies, in savannas, and at the edges of damp thickets, often growing with Big Bluestem grass and Tall Coreopsis.

Cup Plant
Silphium perfoliatum
Aster or Daisy Family

Another of the large, coarse composite plants, Cup Plant derives its common name from the fused bases of its opposite leaves that form a cup often filled with rain water. Its 4-angled stems are typically 4 to 5 feet tall but can grow to 9 feet. From July to September, large, open, rangy heads of flowers bloom on many-branched flowering stems.

Cup Plant ranges from Ontario across to the Dakotas down to Georgia and over to Oklahoma.

Compass Plant; Rosin-weed
Silphium laciniatum
Aster or Daisy Family

Compass Plant is so named because its flat leaves orient themselves vertically from north to south. This orientation may protect fully exposed plants from overheating with the east/west movement of the sun on hot prairies. The leaves are alternate or basal and deeply, pinnately lobed. Rough and bristly, they extend up the stems that can be 3 to 10 feet tall. Late summer and early fall flowers occur along the stem and at the top in heads that can have short stalks or no stalks at all.

Found on priaries and moist meadows and in railroad ditches, Compass Plant grows from southern Michigan west to North Dakota and south to Oklahoma and Texas. It is very rare and local in the eastern part of our area but widespread westward.

Prairie-dock
Silphium terebinthinaceum
Aster or Daisy Family

Standing as sentinels in the prairie, Prairie Dock is one of the best indicators for the possible presence of other choice wet prairie species. With flowering stems up to 12 feet tall, these plants have very distinctive large basal leaves. Almost spade-shaped, coarse, and rough, the basal leaves grow stiffly erect from a large, woody taproot. Flowering stalks, by contrast, are leafless or have leaves only near the base, and the flowers themselves seem sparse and surprisingly small for the stalk's height and the plant's enormous leaves.

Prairie Dock occurs primarily on moist prairies, in fens, or on railroad embankments. Found in many counties in the south of our region, Prairie Dock extends further north but not as far west as other silphiums.

fwc

fwc

Closed Gentian; Bottle Gentian
Gentiana andrewsii
Gentian Family

White Closed Gentian
Gentiana andrewsii f. *albiflora*
Gentian Family

The most common of several species of bottle gentians in the Great Lakes region, this is one of our latest blooming showy flowers outside the daisy family. Multiple stems from the same crown reach heights up to 2 feet and produce flowers in September ranging in color from purple/blue to sky blue or white .

Arranged in tiered clusters, the bottle-like flowers appear at first to be brightly colored buds. Closer examination, however, shows them to be complicated folded and pleated flowers above a platform of bract-like leaves. Bumblebees stand on the leaves and insert their feet into the tips of the flowers, exerting pressure that causes the flowers to open. The bees enter and the flower closes entrapping them temporarily, showering them with pollen, and thus promoting pollination.

Widely distributed throughout the United States and Canada, this perennial gentian occurs on moist prairies, in wet meadows, on streambanks, and in marsh borders. The white form is rarer than the blue and hybridizes on prairies with the White Prairie Gentian, *G. alba*.

194

fwc

Prairie Gentian
Gentiana puberulenta
Gentian Family

Prairie Gentian is one of our showiest but least seen plants. Essentially invisible in the absence of sunlight, its closed, funnel-shaped, tubular flower will open into a showy, star-shaped, deep to sky blue beauty with only a few minutes of bright sun, reclosing with passing clouds.

A perennial that grows primarily on slightly acid to neutral prairies and sands, this non-fringed gentian varies in height from 10 to 20 inches with lance-shaped, rather stiff, shiny green leaves. Found from western New York and Ontario west to Minnesota and North Dakota and south very locally to Georgia, Kansas, and eastern Colorado, it is now very rare in the eastern portion of its range but becoming more frequent on the prairies of the Great Plains.

Jack Pine Plains; Pine, Oak, Aspen Forest

fwc

Our Jack Pine Plains forests contain Jack Pines as well as other pines and oaks, White Birch, Red Maple, and aspen. These plants fall into the category of sun-loving, shade intolerant pioneer trees. Such a forest usually follows a meadow or shrubby successional stage. In their long process of progression to climax vegetation, these forests are but temporary stages since the conditions of shade their occupants create prevents their own seedlings from surviving beneath their canopy. Instead, other species' seedlings, more shade tolerant, survive beneath them and eventually supplant them. The mix of species that develops on a given spot depends upon the texture and fertility of the soil, depth to the water table, latitude and elevation, and temperature extremes, but Jack Pine and oaks dominate.

In a major portion of our region, large beds of deep sands and gravels prevail, deposited by the relatively recent events of Pleistocene glaciation. At the time of early European immi-

gration and exploration in these regions, the land was mainly forested, much of it by grand stands of the magnificent White Pine. White Pine being one of the world's finest softwoods, this forest spawned a lumbering era that practiced cut, slash, and burn lumbering on a vast scale. Following the careless lumbering techniques of the era, vast accidental wildfires swept our region devastating human habitations and wildlife, burning out the humus, and reducing the sand plains to the equivalent of raw sand beds. The natural adaptation of Jack Pine to fire allowed it to take advantage of the lumber era burns and colonize these plains. Before lumbering, Jack Pine was confined largely to Great Lakes shoreline dunes and sands or occurred only very locally on natural burn areas inland.

Jack Pines mature at a very young age. Even stems only a few feet tall can bear cones. The lower seed-bearing cones of Jack Pine typically do not open and shed seed in the manner of most pines. Rather, the seeds remain viable

for a long period and if, during that time, a fast-moving ground fire sweeps the area, the cones, affected by the brief but high temperatures, slowly open their scales releasing the winged seeds. Thus, almost as the burned, raw soil starts to cool, it is heavily seeded with Jack Pine seeds allowing that species a head-start in pioneering the newly burned-over soil. This sometimes results in such dense stands of young Jack Pine that almost nothing can grow beneath, and the trees themselves never achieve normal size. But this behavior enabled a vast series of "Jack Pine barrens" to develop across parts of central and Upper Michigan, Wisconsin, and Minnesota. Fostered by repeated fires, Jack Pine dominated these sand plains for a time after the 1800s lumber era. It is on these open plains with scattered Jack Pines in northern Lower Michigan that one may encounter the rare Kirtland's Warbler.

More recently, with forest fire protection, sufficient time and humus have accumulated to allow the process of plant succession to play its part. In some spots White Pine, in others oaks, White Birch, Quaking Aspen, or various combinations of these have developed, interspersed among the Jack Pine. The decaying needles or leaves of most of these species form humic acids. Regardless of the pH of underlying soils, the rather sterile surface layers tend to be acid.

In early stages, the thin, scraggly nature of the Jack Pine tree allows much light to reach the forest floor. Clearings resulting from the vagaries of wind-blown seed are common. In the clearings, many old field and prairie species may mingle with pioneer forest species. It may be surprising, but not uncommon, to find Indian-pipe, normally considered an old forest, deep humus plant, to be abundant among the grasses and shrubs of this stage. Trailing-arbutus, a sun-lover, may appear as well in clearings, on mossy exposed banks, or in open shade and persist until deep shade develops. Many species follow this same pattern.

In southern and western portions of our coverage area, the dominant pioneer tree on sands may be a species of oak – Red (*Quercus rubra*), White (*Q. alba*), or Bur (*Q. macrocarpa*) – rather than Jack Pine. Their growth may be slow and stunted on these dry, sterile sands and the progress toward forested stands further slowed by ground fires, grazing of native animals, or pasturing. Grazed or burned oak woods may create a savanna type vegetation of grasses and some meadow or prairie herbs in the dappled light. In more moist locales, the pioneer forests may be dominated about equally by oaks, Red Maple, and Quaking or Bigtooth Aspen (*Populus grandidentata*). Fewer prairie species occur, but many of the same species as in Jack Pine or oak savanna may be present. With wetter conditions, however, progress toward a closed canopy, denser forest moves more quickly as does the entire successional process. Large areas of northeastern Michigan and southern Ontario bear such forests today. In these and in very mature Jack Pine forests, succession eventually leads to a White Pine stage that has, in places, been documented to last from 250 to 500 years or more before giving way to the regional climax forest of Beech-Sugar Maple or other deciduous forest.

Jack Pine plains and the other characteristic pioneer forests on these deep sands harbor a limited number of plant species, most of them also found in other habitats. Characteristic plants include Lowbush Blueberry, Huckleberry (*Gaylussacia*), Trailing-arbutus, Slender Ladies'-tresses, Pink Lady's-slippers, Puccoon, Three-toothed Cinquefoil, Birdfoot Violet, Butterfly-weed, various shrubby willows, Big and Little Bluestem grasses, as well as numerous lichens and mosses. But change in most habitats is continuous. Eventually the characteristic pioneer species of these forests become mixed with, compete with, and eventually give way to species better adapted than their seedlings to the conditions the pioneer forest has created. The invaders become the next vegetational stage.

Bellwort; Merrybells
Uvularia sessilifolia
Lily Family

"Wort" is an Anglo-Saxon term meaning "plant." True to its common name, the small, creamy yellow, bell-shaped flowers of this plant hang down on the underside of the stem, fading to white as they mature. The delicate, weakly branched, arching stems bear mostly 1 to 3 blossoms each between April and mid-June, spreading more after flowering. Arising from underground runners, the stems do not form clumps but rather large colonies of scattered plants.

Bellwort is the most delicate of our natives in the genus *Uvularia*. Occurring in some districts and not others, it ranges from New Brunswick west to North Dakota south to Alabama, Georgia, and Missouri.

Trailing-arbutus
Epigaea repens
Heath Family

A superb, delicate fragrance characterizes this early spring bloomer whose flowers may sometimes be located under snow or leaves by their sweet odor. White-tipped with pink or deep pink throughout, the blossoms appear from mid-April to early June. The clusters of flared tubular flowers are borne on matted runners among the large, oval, rough-textured leaves.

Occurring only in early stages of succession, Trailing-arbutus is reputed to be more rare than it really is. It prefers bright diffused light, so as the tree canopy produces more shade, old colonies expire while new colonies develop in more open spots. Most attempts to cultivate this species fail, and picking damages the delicate roots severely. Preferring raw, intensely acid, somewhat sterile habitats, it ranges from Florida to Mississippi north to southern New England, southeast New York, Pennsylvania, W. Virginia, and Ohio.

200

Pink Lady's-slipper
Cypripedium acaule
Orchid Family

Probably the most frequent orchid in our region, Pink Lady's-slipper, also called Moccasin-flower, is deemed stemless because its short stem is underground and therefore unseen. Only leaves and flower scapes grow above ground. Oblong and round at the ends, the 2 basal leaves are strongly ribbed. The usually solitary flowers bloom between May and late June depending on latitude and soil temperature. Typically pink or lavender but occasionally quite red or pure white, this species differs from our other lady's-slippers in having a longitudinal rather than a round opening in its dominant lip.

Widespread throughout eastern North America, Pink Lady's-slipper is abundant in Jack Pine plains, usually in shaded, humus-rich areas. Able to grow with varying amounts of water, it is also frequent in other intensely acid habitats such as oak woods, peat bogs, rock crevices, and outcroppings.

Birdfoot Violet
Viola pedata
Violet Family

Birdfoot Violet is easily identified by its leaves, its flowers, and its habitat. The much divided leaves all arise from the base of the plant. Vaguely reminiscent of a bird's foot, they resemble the leaves of only one other violet in our region, the Prairie Violet. Also distinctive are the large, flat, pansy-like flowers that bloom from April to early June and the plant's occurrence in dry, sandy soils. Held on stalks above the leaves, the blossoms are typically lavender or lilac in color although white and pale blue forms are known. A bicolored form with dark violet upper petals is very rare in our area but common southward.

Largely absent in the extreme northern part of our region, Birdfoot Violet is found from New Hampshire and Ontario across to Michigan and Minnesota south to Florida, Texas, and Kansas.

Sheep-laurel; Lambkill
Kalmia angustifolia
Heath Family

This slender shrub with thin, evergreen leaves rarely grows more than 3 feet tall. A plant of bog borders, disturbed peatlands, and low, peaty wet sands, especially in the Jack Pine plains of Michigan, Sheep-laurel will grow in sun or shade but blooms best in bright light. Its typically mountain-laurel-like flowers appear in June and July, a month later than those of the related Bog-laurel that prefers "wet feet." Rosier in color than its bog cousin, Sheep-laurel displays loose clusters of blossoms along the upper part of its stem below the season's new growth. Color forms include rose, red, dark purple, and white.

The leaves of this species, like those of all *Kalmias*, are considered poisonous to animals and humans. Occurring usually in whorls of 3, they are scattered up the stem with a terminating shoot above the uppermost blossoms.

In the Great Lakes region, Sheep-laurel is largely confined to northeastern Lower Michigan and Ontario. Eastward its distribution extends into New England and south locally into the Carolina mountains. A botanical variety of it grows commonly onto the Southeastern Coastal Plain.

Hill's Thistle
Cirsium hillii
Aster or Daisy Family

This deep-rooted perennial thistle is of low physical stature, usually reaching heights of only 10 to 20 inches. During its first year of growth, Hill's Thistle produces only a basal rosette of leaves. In the second year and annually thereafter, the flowering stalk appears with its rose-pink, spiny flower head. Unlike the corresponding parts of most thistle species, the prickles on the leaf margins of this form are rather soft and the lobes of the leaves are shallow.

Occurring in sandy soil, Hill's Thistle ranges from Ontario to Manitoba southward to Iowa, Indiana, and Illinois. Unreported of late in the south part of our region, it is rare and local on our Jack Pine plains and gravelly dry prairies.

Common Blackberry
Rubus allegheniensis
Rose Family

This highly variable species is a common prickly bramble of drier fields and Jack Pine clearings. Its large, straggly stems feature large, somewhat curved deciduous thorns that love flesh. Arching downward, the stems of Common Blackberry root wherever they touch the ground, often forming large bramble patches. From May through July, the plants display attractive white flowers. Beginning in late July and continuing through early September, the purple-black fruits ripen, varying from year to year and sometimes from plant to plant in flavor. Often confused with black raspberries, blackberry fruits differ in being more solid and not crumbling.

Common Blackberry can be found from New Brunswick and southern Quebec to Minnesota south to Nova Scotia, New England, Long Island, Maryland, upland North Carolina and Tennessee, and Missouri.

203

Low Bindweed
Calystegia spithamaea
Morning-glory Family

Often seen along sandy roadsides in Jack Pine country, Low Bindweed does not usually climb like most of its family members. Its erect shortened stem, somewhat woody at the base, ends in a stalk of leaves that may twine slightly at the tip. The leaves themselves are often downy. Flowering occurs from late May into July with 1 to 3 morning-glory flowers per stem. Most often white, the blossoms open on stalks extending from the axils of the lower leaves and, at up to 2 inches across, may appear conspicuously large for the size of the plant.

Low Bindweed occupies Jack Pine plains, dunes, and other gravelly soils. In Canada, it grows in southern Quebec and Ontario's Thunder Bay District. Its U.S. distribution extends from Minnesota south to Delaware, Maryland, the District of Columbia, upland Virginia, Tennessee, and Iowa.

Sundrops
Oenothera perennis
Evening-primrose Family

Evening-primroses derive their name from their flowers, many of which open at dusk and remain open until morning. Sundrops, however, is diurnal – it blooms in the morning, the flowers lasting through the day. One or more erect leafy flowering stalks arise to about a foot from a basal rosette of leaves from late May into August. The tips of the stalks and buds may nod, but the flowers become erect as they open.

This rather small species of sundrop occurs in a variety of habitats, both dry and moist, including moist depressions in Jack Pines. Its wide area of distribution includes Newfoundland to eastern Manitoba south to Nova Scotia, New England, Long Island, Delaware, eastern Virginia, upland to Georgia, West Virginia, Ohio, Indiana, and Missouri.

Frostweed; Rockrose
Helianthemum canadense
Rockrose Family

In freezing weather, Frostweed often exhibits ice crystal formation within outer stem cracks at the base of its stems – hence, its common name. Growing to heights of 10 to 20 inches, this erect perennial produces 2 kinds of flowers. A few large-petaled blossoms like that pictured open at the ends of the branches. Among the large flowers and at the bases of the leaves along the stem occur clusters of smaller, self-fertilizing flowers with few or no petals. The latter never open.

Frostweed may be found in dry sandy woods and on dunes of the northeastern United States and adjacent Canada south to North Carolina and Kentucky.

Slender Ladies'-tresses
Spiranthes lacera
Orchid Family

Slender Ladies'-tresses bloom in late July and early August when Lowbush Blueberries ripen. It can occur in any sandy old field in our region or on dunes, but it is particularly abundant on Jack Pine plains where sandy bare areas and moss beds free of competing grasses harbor the greatest numbers.

For most of the year, the plant is only a basal rosette of soft, apple-green leaves resembling an unmarked rattlesnake plantain orchid. In early July, a very slender flower stalk grows from 10 to 18 inches tall with a few barely visible leaf-like bracts and a single twisted rank of pearly white flowers at the top. Vaguely reminiscent of braids in their arrangement, the tiny flowers display a dark green blotch on the floor of their lip (lowermost petal).

So slender and delicate that they often go unnoticed, Slender Ladies'-tresses are found throughout the Great Lakes region but more abundantly in some districts than others. The species ranges far south and east of our region also.

Smooth False Foxglove
Aureolaria flava
Snapdragon Family

Aureolarias are hemi-parasitic, usually on oaks. While green and photosynthetic, they are thought to obtain food and/or growth hormones from their host.

Smooth False Foxglove grows 2 to 4 feet tall, displaying loose pyramidal clusters of "foxglove" flowers from July to September. Yellow in color as the name *flava* denotes, they open only a few at a time, usually in the presence of buds of varying sizes. Of the 3 native false foxgloves, this is the only one with entirely smooth fruits. Dried fruiting stalks from the previous season frequently persist among the stems of the current season. Found most frequently in the south of our region, Smooth False Foxglove occurs from Maine to Minnesota south to Georgia and Alabama.

Downy Rattlesnake Plantain
Goodyera pubescens
Orchid Family

Downy Rattlesnake Plantain grows in almost any type of wooded cover with acid surface conditions. Its rosettes of evergreen leaves, each with a distinctive network of white veins, form at the ends of creeping rhizomes. The more vigorous rosettes, when mature, produce a summer flowering spike up to 15 inches tall with a cylinder of numerous small, downy, green and white flowers. The partial lip of each flower bears a curious pouch at its base. After seed production, the rhizome branches, each branch forming a new rosette before the old rosette dies. Over a period of time, a single plant may produce a large colony of rosettes, only a few of which will bloom in a given year.

Found from Quebec and Ontario south to Georgia and Alabama, this species is generally more common in the south in our region.

207

Gray Goldenrod
Solidago nemoralis
Aster or Daisy Family

Smaller and more delicate than many of its relatives, Gray Goldenrod features hairs on its stems and leaves that give the plant its grayish appearance. Its numerous narrow leaves are gradually reduced in size toward the narrow flower head. Found in clumps of 2 to 10, the flower spikes commence blooming in late mid-summer, ahead of most other goldenrods, with inflorescences that often appear to tip or lean.

Gray Goldenrod is conspicuous along roadsides in Jack Pine plains and on gravelly hillsides. Preferring sterile, sandy, dry soil, it ranges from Georgia to Texas north to southeastern Canada, Minnesota, and North Dakota.

Wintergreen; Teaberry
Gaultheria procumbens
Heath Family

Wintergreen can form a conspicuous carpet in moist to dry shaded pine woods and mixed pine deciduous forest. Extremely abundant in the northern pine woods of our region, this low plant grows only 3 to 4 inches tall with 5 to 6 glossy, leathery green leaves that may assume a bronzy red tone in winter. In July and August, small white bell-like flowers with united petals hang in clusters from the leaf axils. Once pollinated, they produce bright red, fleshy berries that may persist for a year or more on the plant. The base of each berry displays a 5-pointed, fleshy flower scar.

Both leaves and fruits of the Wintergreen plant possess a delicious wintergreen flavor. Found frequently under conifers, it grows from Newfoundland to Manitoba south to Nova Scotia, New England, Georgia, Alabama, Wisconsin, and Minnesota.

fwc

fwc

Sands and gravels deposited by Pleistocene glaciation or by wind action near the Great Lakes shores abound in our region. Through the vagaries of chance, location, and the various geological processes extant here combined with the actions of man, both ancient and modern, and animals (i.e. bison), the plant species that invaded our deep sandy deposits gave rise to shore and dune plants as well as sand (dry) prairie or Jack Pine plains vegetation. These habitats, through the process of plant succession, may later progress into forests of oak, aspen, some Red Maple, and birch. This in turn may succeed to a White Pine dominated stage and eventually into deciduous climax forest southward or northern coniferous forest northward. On the more extensive deep dry sand deposits, however, successional progress is very slow. If, as was apparently common in the past, these lands are subjected to repeated fires, either natural (lightening) or man-caused, the burning maintains prairie vegetation for long periods. Although prairie vegetation as a true climax formation occurs only west of the coverage area of this book, European pioneers found here extensive dry sand prairie, especially in western Lower Michigan and westward in Illinois and Wisconsin.

In the early history of our region, many people homesteaded on some of this dry land as well as northward on the recently lumbered and burned regions of the formerly extensive White Pine forest. Because of the very dry sandy soil, harsh climate, and short growing season, many of these farms failed after a few years and were abandoned to go back to nature. In the process, on these "old fields" much sand prairie vegetation invaded. To this day, in places such as Allegan or Newaygo Counties in western Lower Michigan and elsewhere, abandoned farm fields produce patches of sand prairie of considerable richness.

Prairie plants such as Big and Little Bluestem grasses, Indian Grass, hawkweed, Chicory, and Mullein dominate the land. Tall Coreopsis, coneflower, Blazing-star, lupines, and goldenrods give the prairies a blaze of color in sum-

mer, while such rarities in our region as Downy Gentian, White Prairie Gentian, and Prickly-pear occur only rarely but are more frequently met westward. Of course damper soils occur near streams, in swales and depressions, and near ponds and lakes. Wet meadow and lake plain mesic prairie species may occur locally in these special habitats and blend with the drier prairie vegetation.

Over a large area of central and northern Michigan and Wisconsin, clear-cut lumbering followed by fire destroyed the humus and reduced the soils to open dry sands. In these extensive areas, a fire adapted tree, Jack Pine, a relatively small, thin, open pine that does not create the dense shade of the White Pine, quickly invaded and became the dominant pioneer tree. Openings in the the Jack Pine forest allowed some prairie species to invade and persist for long periods. Thus, while plants of Jack Pine plains are not strictly considered as prairie vegetation, some sand prairie plants may be encountered there.

Today, unfortunately, the richer prairie soils are mostly cultivated or in tree plantations where natural fire is severely curtailed. Without fire, humus accumulates rapidly, retains moisture, and allows invasion of non-prairie species, speeding plant succession processes. The result is that our prairies have grown smaller and our prairie species have become quite rare.

Seeking to preserve part of our pioneer prairie heritage, various conservation groups who hold prairie preserves use prescribed burns to hold back natural succession and attempt to maintain prairie plants.

fwc

Wild Lupine
Lupinus perennis
Pea Family

In flower from April to July, Wild Lupine is one of our showiest members of the Pea Family, particularly when in large populations. Spreading by underground roots, the members of such a population may all be the product of a single plant.

When newly opened, the usually blue-purple flowers of Wild Lupine have a creamy marking on the mouth that aids insects in locating nectar. As the flowers age, the marking changes to a reddish color that is less visible to insects, hence only the freshest flowers are pollinated. The flowers can be up to 1 inch long, occurring sometimes in white or rose to pink shades, and the fruits are bean pods.

Wild Lupine reaches heights up to 1 foot. Its leaves feature 7 to 11 leaflets radiating out from a common point of attachment like the spokes of a wheel. Our native variety grows in sandy soils from southwest Maine to New York and Minnesota south to Iowa, Illinois, Ohio, W. Virginia, and Florida.

jrw

Prairie Smoke; Prairie Avens
Geum triflorum
Rose Family

Prairie Smoke is most distinguishable as flowers mature into wind-dispersed clusters of fruits, the "smoke" of its common name referring to feathery masses of "hairs" evident at that time. Each plume equates with a seed of its distant relative strawberry. Developed from the ovary and the style, each plume ultimately catches the wind which aids in transporting it to a new habitat.

This low perennial has softly hairy stems with basal leaves divided into many wedge-shaped segments. From April to June, nodding, straw-colored to purplish blossoms occur on simple stems usually in groups of 3, *triflorum* meaning three-flowered. As the flowers develop their fruits, they straighten on the stem, the seed-head being fully erect.

Found in sandy prairie soils and calcareous gravels, Prairie Smoke ranges from the shores of Lake Huron to Alberta south to northern Illinois, Iowa, Nebraska, and Montana.

Wild Teasel
Dipsacus fullonum
Teasel Family

Wild Teasel derives its common name from the use of its spiny heads by women to tease their hair and in the woolen industry to comb wool. Naturalized from Europe, this biennial has branched, square stems with prickles at the stem angles and along the leaf margins. It reaches heights of 5 feet and more and can form large, conspicuous colonies.

Pink flowers are evident between June and October, but this plant is most easily identified in fruit. Its cylindrical fruit clusters with their very long spines provide a showy presence in the winter landscape as well as in floral arrangements when dry.

A plant typically growing along roadsides and railroads, in fields, and on heavy, open, disturbed ground, Wild Teasel occurs from western Quebec and western New England to Ontario and Michigan south to North Carolina, Tennessee, and Missouri.

218

Yellow Hawkweed; King Devil
Hieracium piloselloides
Aster or Daisy Family

Orange Hawkweed; Devil's Paintbrush
Hieracium aurantiacum
Aster or Daisy Family

The Yellow and Orange Hawkweeds are among the most common and easily recognized plants along dry sandy roadsides and lakeshores, in old fields, along railroad tracks, in meadows with native plants, and in every kind of waste place. Their single, usually leafless stems arise from a basal rosette of somewhat hairy elongated leaves, reaching heights of 1 to 2 feet. In mid- to late summer, clusters of flowering heads, each up to 1 inch wide, top the stems, differing only in color. Where the two grow together, however, they are known to hybridize with each other, producing bicolored (red on the tips, yellow at the base) flowers. Orange Hawkweed consistently produces flat-growing stems (stolons) from the base of the plant and is coarsely hairy. Yellow Hawkweed is smoother and rarely produces stolons.

Introduced from Europe in the Northeast, both species are aggressive invaders of disturbed soil and have quickly expanded west and south, initially by seeds and then locally spreading by creeping horizontal stems. Orange Hawkweed grows from Newfoundland to Minnesota south to Nova Scotia, New England, Virginia, Ohio, Indiana, Illinois, and Iowa. Known formerly as *H. florentinum*, Yellow Hawkweed is absent from Indiana and Illinois in our region, ranging from Newfoundland to Ontario south to Nova Scotia, New England, Virginia, Ohio, Michigan, and Iowa.

Ox-eye Daisy
Chrysanthemum leucanthemum
Aster or Daisy Family

The phrase "loves me, loves me not" brings to mind the Ox-eye Daisy for large numbers of people, but among botanists this species is known for its long Latin name meaning, simply, "yellow and white flower." Blooming from June to August, each daisy is actually numerous white ray flowers with elongated petals surrounding a mass of yellow disk flowers with tiny petals. Topping stems up to 20 inches tall, the white flowers serve to attract pollinators to the yellow, seed-bearing disk flowers. Leaves typically have large teeth and small narrow lobes on each side.

Another introduction from Europe, Ox-eye Daisy occurs thoroughly naturalized across North America along roadsides and railroads, in fields and clearings, and on waste ground. It is the wild ancestor of the showy garden favorite Shasta Daisy.

Purple Coneflower
Echinacea pallida
Aster or Daisy Family

Purple Coneflower is a signature plant of the prairie habitat commonly found throughout its native range – Michigan to Nebraska south to Alabama, Louisiana, and Texas. In June and July it can dominate the landscape with its pale lavender, drooping ray flowers topping almost leafless stalks that arise from a clump of basal leaves. It is pollinated by bees and butterflies. When all the petals have withered, the head forms a persistent cone of stiff, short, spine-like projections. Seed-eating birds like goldfinches can pick the nutritious black seeds from between the spines. Unlike their native relatives, cultivated forms of coneflower grow in clumps and have larger stem leaves and more colorful flowers.

Prickly-pear
Opuntia humifusa
Cactus Family

Rare in the Great Lakes region, Prickly-pear grows close to the ground, its branched and flattened stem segments, "pads," potentially forming a carpet several feet across. Longer spines arise from among small, raised clusters of tiny, barbed, vicious spines called glochids on the fleshy segments. Many-petaled, showy yellow flowers resembling water-lilies top the stems in June and July, followed by reportedly edible, pulpy red fruits.

Prickly-pear grows in arid sandy and sunny locations from Massachusetts to Minnesota south to South Carolina, upland Georgia, Alabama, Mississippi, Missouri, and Oklahoma.

Common St. John's-wort
Hypericum perforatum
St. John's-wort Family

Orange-yellow flowers with minute black dots on the petals are typical for this species. Naturalized from Europe, Common St. John's-wort has spread over much of the United States and Canada, frequently as an unwelcome addition to the landscape. Plants achieve heights of 1 to 1½ feet with opposite, smooth-margined leaves dotted with tiny pits or glands characteristic of this family. The glandular dots, filled with oils, are translucent and somewhat visible when held to light. Flowering occurs throughout the summer, the terminal blossom rather than the lower one on each angled stem opening first.

Capable of growing in a variety of habitats, St. John's-wort is difficult to eradicate, particularly because its long flowering period produces so many seeds.

Goat's-beard; Vegetable Oyster; Salsify
Tragopogon dubius
Aster or Daisy Family

This goat's-beard is one of two yellow-flowered species that grow in our area; a third species produces purple flowers. Wherever 2 or 3 species occur together, hybrids in all combinations are possible – in fact, they are a midwest phenomenon.

Naturalized from Europe, this stout, 3-foot biennial develops from roots that resemble parsnips. Flowering from July to October, Goat's-beard produces large, solitary, many-flowered heads that open in the late morning and close in the evening. Rays of the central flowers are about half as long as those of the outer flowers.

The name Goat's-beard refers to the mature fruit cluster. Spherical in shape and up to 4 inches across, it resembles the smaller dandelion fruit cluster. Each tiny fruit bears a seed with a terminal, plume-like parachute that aids in seed dispersal.

A plant of roadsides, fields, and other waste places, Goat's-beard ranges from New York to Washington south to Virginia, Illinois, Texas, and California. Native Americans coagulated the milky juice of the stems and leaves of this plant for use as chewing gum. The seed heads are sometimes used for decoration, but they must be sprayed with hair spray or clear varnish to prevent their falling apart.

Goats-rue; Rabbit-pea
Tephrosia virginiana
Pea Family

Aside from its unique flower color – yellowish white and purple – and its flower shape suggestive of sweet-peas, the best descriptor for Goats-rue is "hoary," referring to the presence of long silky whitish hairs on its leaves and stems. Almost woody, the leafy stems grow to heights of 1 to 2 feet in discrete clumps. In mid-summer, clusters of flowers appear at the tips of the stems, to be followed with typical bean-like pods.

An inhabitant of sandy plains and dry woodlands, Goats-rue can be found from Florida to Texas north to southern New Hampshire, Massachusetts, New York, southern Ontario, southern Michigan, southern Wisconsin, Missouri, and Oklahoma.

Musk Mallow
Malva moschata
Mallow Family

A relative of the cotton plant, Musk Mallow reportedly has a musk-scented aroma. The many branches of this showy perennial can be erect or somewhat reclining. Upper stem leaves typically feature 5 to 7 parts deeply cut like a feather while basal and lower leaves can have 5 broad lobes. White or pink flowers 2 inches or more in diameter occur in loose clusters at the branch tips from July to September, their stamen arrangement resembling a bottle brush in the center of the blossom as in their relative, the hollyhock.

Musk Mallow ranges from Newfoundland to northern New England and less commonly westward from Ontario to Nebraska south to Delaware, Maryland, and Tennessee. A popular choice for gardens, it is another species naturalized from Europe.

223

fwc

224

taf

Wild-bergamot
Monarda fistulosa
Mint Family

A variable and very common member of the Mint Family, this species also bears the common name Horse Mint for the distinctive, suggestive "aroma" of the entire plant. The soft, velvety texture of Wild-bergamot differentiates it from similar species; but like most mints, this plant exhibits square stems and opposite leaves. Reaching heights up to 4 feet, its many gray-green stems stand erect with lance-shaped, toothed leaves of the same color.

Mid- to late summer brings compact, head-like clusters of 2-lipped flowers at the tips of the branches or in angles between the upper leaves and stems. Although white-flowered individuals may be found, shades of lilac to pink occur most commonly.

Dry, sandy soils of roadsides, clearings, thickets, open hillsides, and woods borders are typical sites for Wild-bergamot. Its wide area of distribution extends from southwest Quebec to western New England to Minnesota south to Maryland, upland Georgia and Alabama, Louisiana, and eastern Texas.

Common Mullein
Verbascum thapsus
Snapdragon Family

Mullein
Verbascum phlomoides
Snapdragon Family

Familiar tall weeds of dry habitats, biennial mulleins form large rosettes of grayish green leaves in their first year. Densely felted in both species, the leaves become reduced as they extend along the second year's flowering stem.

Both species produce flowers on tall spikes, Common Mullein from June to September, Mullein in July and August. The yellow flowers of Common Mullein barely open. More dense on their spike, they nevertheless don't provide the show of Mullein blossoms. Also yellow, the latter are more scattered on their stalk and more open, sometimes as large as 1 inch across. The rod-like fruit spikes of Common Mullein frequently over-winter.

Mullein (*V. phlomoides*) usually is the taller of the two plants, reaching striking heights of 8 feet. A field of this species can provide a memorable sight.

Plants of roadsides, clearings, old fields, and disturbed grounds, mulleins have spread extensively along interstate highways. Both natives of the Old World, Common Mullein grows throughout the eastern United States while Mullein is local from Maine to Minnesota south to North Carolina, Kentucky, and Iowa.

Red Clover
Trifolium pratense
Pea Family

Imported from Europe and naturalized throughout much of North America, Red Clover was originally introduced for agricultural purposes. Today, its importance as a livestock food and for soil enrichment assure continued cultivation.

Clover plants can be erect or partially reclined. The alternate leaves of this species vary in the length of their stalks – they become shorter or non-existent closer to the top of the plant – and feature 3 finely toothed leaflets each. Dense, magenta flower heads first appear in May, continuing to bloom sporadically for the remainder of the summer. Each flower, as in most members of the Pea Family, structurally resembles that of the sweet-pea in miniature.

Star-thistle; Spotted Knapweed
Centaurea maculosa
Aster or Daisy Family

A biennial or short-lived perennial, Star-thistle exhibits wiry stems up to 3 feet tall. Its narrowly pinnately cut (feather-like) leaves, a characteristic grayish green in color, mound near the ground. The tubular flowers can range from an almost white light pink to deep lavender pink, occurring in clustered heads up to 1 inch wide. Also especially characteristic are the deeply divided edges of the leafy bracts surrounding each head of flowers. Both blooming and non-blooming stalks may exist in the same population of plants during the June to August flowering period.

An introduced Mediterranean weed, Star-thistle spreads rapidly in sterile, sandy, disturbed areas and has become a serious pastureland pest westward. It ranges from Quebec to British Columbia south to Nova Scotia, New England, Virginia, Tennessee, Missouri, and Kansas.

fwc

Butterfly-weed
Asclepias tuberosa
Milkweed Family

Among the milkweeds, Butterfly-weed is a standout for several reasons in addition to its usually brilliant orange flower color. Its alternate rather than opposite leaves distinguish it from other family members, and it is our only milkless milkweed, its juices being clear.

The rough hairy stems of this species arise in clusters to a height of 1 to 3 feet from a large, deep tap root. The erect to sprawling stems bear many narrow leaves and broad flower heads at the branch tips with smaller heads at the joints of leaves and stem. Flower color is variable from yellow to orange-red to red, most commonly some shade of orange. Each flower displays the characteristic milkweed shape: a ring of somewhat reflexed sepals and petals with a crown of hood-like structures attached to the filaments and bearing peculiar curved horns from within. Plants bloom from June to August in the Great Lakes region.

Butterfly-weed occurs from Arizona to Maine and Ontario to Florida.

jrw

Common Milkweed
Asclepias syriaca
Milkweed Family

This coarse, summer-flowering, native perennial can attain heights up to 6 feet. In addition to its many seeds formed each fall, Common Milkweed often spreads aggressively by horizontal stems beneath the ground's surface. The dull purple flowers appear in spherical clusters at the base of each leaf pair along the upper half of the stem between June and August. Like other family members, Common Milkweed displays complex flowers, each with horn-like projections arising from the nectar-holding cups. The function of this projection is unknown. In the fall, large, warty, pod-shaped fruits split open along one side at maturity, releasing masses of seeds bearing silky hairs that carry the seeds on the wind like miniature parachutes.

The species name *syriaca* literally means "from Syria." Swedish botanist Carl Linnaeus applied that name in the eighteenth century under a then common misconception as to the plant's origin.

Common Milkweed occurs from western New Brunswick to Saskatchewan south to Georgia, Tennessee, Iowa, and Kansas.

230

Bouncing Bet; Soapwort
Saponaria officinalis
Pink Family

Although less showy than other members of the carnation family, this introduction from Europe has become well established in our region, forming large colonies by means of branching, underground runners. The stems of this 12- to 20-inch perennial appear swollen at the attachment points of its opposite leaves – a family trait. The whitish-pink to pinkish-lavender flowers bloom from July to September, often having twice the usual 5 petals.

Aggressive in the garden and the wild, Bouncing Bet often is found in large beds along railroad embankments and roadsides as well as in other open sandy locales. In moist situations it can be lush. Pioneers rubbed pulverized roots or leaves of this plant with water to make a crude soapy lather, hence the sobriquet Soapwort.

Self-heal
Prunella vulgaris
Mint Family

Introduced from Eurasia, widely dispersed across the continent, and extremely variable, Self-heal is one of our most common members of the Mint Family. As is clearly evident in this photograph, it exhibits the family's characteristic square stem as well as opposite leaves. The dense heads of 2-lipped flowers, usually lavender or pink, are borne in clusters of 3 among leafy bracts. The usual distinctive minty aroma of the plant oils, however, is lacking in this species.

Self-heal, like some other weedy species, has the uncanny ability to adapt to the level of mowing. It may produce its pink to purple 3-flowered clusters when 1 foot tall on an unmowed ditch bank or when only 3 inches tall in a manicured lawn.

231

Yellow Rocket
Barbarea vulgaris
Mustard Family

Yellow Rocket blooms from early spring through summer, but it is perhaps at its best in spring when lack of competition in open areas enables it to cover many acres via abundant seedling growth in recently abandoned fields. Its many stems emerge from a basal clump of glossy, dark green leaves, growing to heights of 1 to 3 feet. The late winter clusters of these leaves frequently find their way onto dinner plates in restaurants featuring wild plants. The bright yellow, 4-petaled flowers occur in clusters at the ends of branches.

Variable and widely distributed, Yellow Rocket occupies fields, waste grounds, cultivated grounds, and roadsides from Newfoundland to Ontario south to Virginia, Ohio, Indiana, Illinois, Missouri, and Kansas. Certain forms are cultivated in Europe.

Yellow Sweet-clover
Melilotus officinalis
Pea Family

Although the individual flowers of this introduced species are quite small, a field of Yellow Sweet-clover with its pleasant aroma can be memorable. Rarely less than 3 feet tall, the plants can tolerate some of the poorest soil conditions.

Sometimes called "green manure," Yellow Sweet-clover, like other Pea Family members, contains nitrogen-fixing bacteria in its roots and is thus useful in enriching poor soil. The 3 leaflets that comprise its leaves are typically twice as long as they are broad. Sweet-pea-like but tiny, the flowers occur in an erect raceme from May to October.

Yellow Sweet-clover grows along roadsides and railroads; in fields, disturbed areas and woods; and on shores and waste places from Quebec to British Columbia south. This and an almost identical white-flowered form, *M. alba*, are natives of Eurasia.

Black-eyed Susan
Rudbeckia hirta
Aster or Daisy Family

One of our showiest native wild-flowers, Black-eyed Susan occupies fields, thickets, and open woods displaying its distinctive yellow daisy flowers from June to October. Averaging 2 feet in height, its hairy, branching stems bear hairy leaves with large teeth. A raised, broadly pyramidal cone of dark brown central florets surrounded by orange-yellow ray flowers give this species its common name.

Black-eyed Susan ranges from western Massachusetts to Illinois south to Georgia and Alabama. Easy and choice to cultivate, it also inhabits many gardens.

Wild Carrot; Queen-Anne's-lace
Daucus carota
Carrot or Parsley Family

Queen-Anne's-lace is perhaps our most common member of the Carrot Family. Frequently seen along roadsides, this biennial grows to 3 feet tall with rough, hairy stems. Its root emits a typical carrot odor that helps differentiate this species from Common Water-hemlock. Flat-topped umbels 2 to 6 inches in diameter bear tiny white flowers, each cluster having at its center a single purple flower thought to act as a decoy in attracting pollinators, predominantly flies and beetles.

An ancestor of the cultivated carrot and naturalized from Europe, Queen-Anne's-lace can be found from Quebec south and west.

233

234

Chicory
Cichorium intybus
Aster or Daisy Family

Mid-summer until frost finds this familiar species blooming in masses along roadsides, in waste places, and in old fields. These introduced biennial plants have few leaves and vary widely in height from just above the ground to 4 feet tall. Up to 2 inches wide, the characteristic blue flower heads of Chicory open in the morning and close late in the day. White and pink forms are rarely seen.

Chicory is now found from coast to coast throughout much of North America. Its taproot, when roasted, is used as an additive in coffee.

Viper's Bugloss; Blueweed
Echium vulgare
Borage Family

Another Old World species now widely naturalized, Viper's Bugloss can survive in the poorest of soils. Its very coarse, biennial plants grow 1 to 2 feet tall, appearing rough and bristly. Sharp, delicate hairs cover all parts of the plant making handling it ill-advised. Beginning in mid-summer and continuing into September, Viper's Bugloss produces a succession of tubular royal blue flowers on continuously elongating, uncoiling branches. As the blossoms age, they fade to pink.

Viper's Bugloss is considered an obnoxious weed in some parts of its range that extends from Quebec to western Ontario south to the North Carolina mountains.

Hairy Vetch
Vicia villosa
Pea Family

Introduced from Europe, Hairy Vetch was once cultivated as a forage crop. Tendrils on its hairy leaves enable it to scramble over grasses and other vegetation in old fields. Throughout the summer, this plant bears drooping, dense racemes of small, violet, sweet-pea-like flowers along only one side of its central axis.

Perhaps poisonous for human consumption, Hairy Vetch occurs in thickets and along roadsides as well as in old fields throughout North America.

236

Butter-and-eggs
Linaria vulgaris
Snapdragon Family

The deep yellow and orange colors of its charming 1-inch, snapdragon-like flowers give Butter-and-eggs its common name. Growing up to 2 feet tall, the usually short and somewhat delicate plants of the species form colonies by means of underground stems. A single rootstock can produce many flowering stems. Butter-and-eggs flowers from June to October, its blossoms opening like a mouth if squeezed laterally.

A perennial introduced from Europe, this plant is related to the garden snapdragon. It grows in open fields and along roadsides across the continent, often the last showy flower blooming in grassy old fields in late autumn.

Evening-primrose
Oenothera biennis
Evening-primrose Family

A biennial, Evening-primrose produces only a flattened basal rosette of leaves up to 1 foot in diameter in its first year following seed germination. During its second and final year, plants 3 to 4 feet tall bloom from June to October. The showy, yellow, 4-petaled flowers, up to 2 inches wide, open in the evening and close by noon.

Evening-primrose varies greatly within its widespread distribution ranging throughout much of North America. Characterized as a noxious weed by many, it is pollinated by night-flying moths whose heads become covered by the sticky threads of yellow pollen.

238

Spotted Bergamot; Horse Mint
Monarda punctata
Mint Family

The species name of this plant, *punctata*, means "dotted or spotted," an appropriate designation for the lavender- or green-colored petals with reddish spots. Blooming from July to October, Horse Mint is most attractive at its mid-summer flowering peak. Plants up to 1½ feet tall display showy opposite gray to white leaves, often reddish or pink streaked, on spikes interrupted by blooms. Both its leaf arrangement and square stems are typical of the Mint Family.

Horse Mint is native in dry, sandy soils from the eastern United States as far west as Arizona and Mexico.

Flowering Spurge
Euphorbia corollata
Spurge Family

The white "petals" of Flowering Spurge are, in fact, tiny modified leaves called bracts comparable to the red leaves of poinsettias to which it is related. Growing up to 2 feet tall, the stems of this species, like all euphorbias, contain a milky sap that can be irritating to human skin. Numerous oval-shaped leaves, dark green in color, occur below the flowers.

Dichotomously forked, the inflorescence of this plant consists of individual flowers no more than $1/4$ inch wide. By the end of the summer, however, the tiny flowers and white leaves can form large arrays, making the plants more showy as the season progresses.

The deep roots of Flowering Spurge produce 1 to several stems each year in dry soils of waste places and clearings and along roadsides. Its wide range extends from Florida to Texas north to New York, southern Ontario, Michigan, Wisconsin, Minnesota, and Nebraska.

Rough Blazing-star
Liatris aspera
Aster or Daisy Family

Blazing-star
Liatris scariosa
Aster or Daisy Family

Blazing-stars, strictly American plants, are among the showiest late summer species of dry, sunny habitats. Linear-lanceolate leaves along the stem and larger basal leaves characterize these plants. In addition to roots, nearly all *Liatris* species develop enlarged, corm-like, underground structures, some more closely resembling a taproot and some round as in both varieties shown here. Bristly, dry parachute hairs on the seeds aid wind-dispersal.

The dense flower heads of August and early September open from the top down, unlike those of most spike-forming plants. Close examination of the cluster of flowers will reveal heads of tiny disk flowers, each with 5 pointed petals and a protruding forked stigma. The ray flowers typical of asters and daisies are absent in *Liatris*.

The two blazing-stars pictured are the most frequently met on dry prairie and Jack Pine forest in our region. Rough Blazing Star occurs from Ohio to North Dakota south to Louisiana and east Texas. It reaches heights of 2 feet with a narrow, almost zigzagged stem and rose-purple flower heads attached on very short stalks or no stalks (sessile).

Blazing-star, once included in *L. aspera* as var. *nieuwlandii* but now considered a separate species, is abundant in old fields and jack pine barrens of Lower Michighan, Wisconsin, Ohio, Illinois, Indiana, and Missouri. Its usually deep purple flowers occur in raceme-like clusters at the top of the stem, not all along it like those of Rough Blazing-star. The heavier stems and more equally sized leaves of Blazing-star also separate the two.

Now widely used in floral arrangements, *Liatris* species are choice cultivated plants for the sunny perennial border and commercial cut flowers.

241

Early Goldenrod
Solidago juncea
Aster or Daisy Family

Like other goldenrods, Early Goldenrod suffers from the common misconception that it causes hay fever. Pollinated by insects and having sticky pollen, goldenrods do not shed pollen into the air. Rather they bloom in late summer and early fall at the same time as the inconspicuous Giant Ragweed with its wind-dispersed pollen that causes allergic reactions.

Early Goldenrod derives its common name from the grayish appearance of small hairs covering its stems and leaves. Up to 3 feet tall, its central flowering stem produces lateral branches quite short for goldenrods, the typical yellow flowers occurring from late June to October. A native found in dry open soil habitats, it ranges from northeastern and central Canada south to southern New England, Delaware, Maryland, and mainly on the Piedmont and upland to Georgia, Tennessee, and Missouri.

Showy Goldenrod
Solidago speciosa
Aster or Daisy Family

With its massive, much branched flower heads, Showy Goldenrod lives up to its common name from late summer into fall. Lacy and yellow, the heads are oval in outline and more conspicuous than those of some goldenrod species because leaves immediately below the spiked inflorescence are small. The numerous, rigid leaves become increasingly larger and more elongate near the base of the plant.

Showy Goldenrod thrives best in the bright light of openings in pine barrens and oak woods and on prairies. Extremely variable in size, it can be 15 inches to 5 or 6 feet tall. One of our most beautiful native flowers, it occurs from North Carolina to Louisiana and Oklahoma north to Massachusetts, New York, Ohio, Michigan, Illinois, and southern Minnesota.

Staghorn Sumac
Rhus typhina
Cashew Family

A native shrub or small tree, Staghorn Sumac is a standout in the fall landscape with compound leaves turning various shades of yellow, orange, purple, and red and bright red fruits in upright panicles that persist into winter. Unlike the drooping white "berries" of Poison Sumac, the red, berry-like drupes of this species are not poisonous. In fact, they reportedly make a refreshing lemonade-like drink when wrapped in cheesecloth and steeped in warm water. Preceding the fruits are tiny, individually inconspicuous, somewhat fleshy greenish flowers.

The "staghorn" designation of this species refers to its large, coarsely hairy twigs reminiscent of deer antlers when "in the velvet." This feature distinguishes it from a smaller, closely related Smooth Sumac (*R. glabra*) that grows in the same habitat.

Staghorn Sumac may form large colonies from underground roots and can be troublesome in cultivated situations. It ranges from the Gaspé Peninsula and Quebec to southern Ontario and Minnesota south to Nova Scotia, New England, North Carolina, Kentucky, Illinois, and Iowa.

Rocky Outcrops, Cliffs, and Alvar

Rocky outcrops, cliffs, and alvar, while occurring in a variety of rock types and exposures, share certain features that make them havens for plants otherwise rare and unusual in a given district.

We have spoken much about plant succession in this book. Most habitats undergo a continuous change in makeup because the plants living at that site grow. Leaves die, fall, accumulate, and decay forming humus. Humus holds more moisture than the original soil did, often forming humic acids and tannins that alter the soil's chemistry. Heavy layers of fresh dead leaves and litter can smother germinating seedlings not adapted to it. As the plants on a site grow vigorously, they produce more shade, another problem for their seedlings to handle. Eventually the seedlings of the original plants on a site cannot tolerate the altered conditions their parent plants have produced. Consequently most species exist in a given spot only briefly until they have altered the site so much by their growth that seedlings of other species invade and gradually take over while the original plants survive by seeding to another spot where geological events have created the open, raw, humusfree, sunny habitat they require. Thus most habitats change and their species makeup changes over time.

On outcrops of rock and steep cliffs, however, successional change is less apparent. A vertical or steep cliff experiences drastic erosional forces of gravity and running water. In many places on cliffs and outcrops, humus washes or falls away almost as fast as it forms. Frost action – from ice forming and expanding in crevices – plus rapid expansion and contraction – from solar heating and rapid cooling of the surface – aided by gravity and the steep slope may cause flaking off of the rock surface exposing new raw rock. Rock slides are frequent. On large areas of outcrop or cliff face, fresh new rock surfaces constantly develop. Succession seldom gets to progress beyond the early stage before one of these events recreates it. Consequently there is always on the rock surface a suitable place for a few seedlings to remain over periods far longer than typical with flatland succession. The harsh environment on this always "new site" seldom supports vast numbers of plants to compete for light, soil, and moisture. But that same freedom from competition may allow plants to survive on these cliffs that could not establish or persist in other habitats within the district because their main habitat was long obliterated by the action of the biota there.

If, in our region, the exposure is northern or heavily shaded and moist and cool, subarctic or arctic species that reached the area by chance or have remained there from a former climate may persist indefinitely. On hot, dry, highly exposed rocks, southern or western species may appear and establish but occur nowhere else in the region.

The chemistry and fertility of the rocks also determine which plant species may grow there, excluding some while permitting others to persist. Limestones tend to release more useful plant nutrients than granites, but they also create alkaline conditions. Granites, often rather nutritionally sterile, may be acidic or alkaline depending upon what minerals are present. Serpentine rocks, rich in heavy metals that kill or stunt many plants, often support limited numbers of species or stunted vegetation. Yet each of these conditions also favors certain specially adapted species, whether they be relict there or simply need those conditions.

In the Great Lakes region, outcrops and cliffs of various rocks attract botanists and rare plant enthusiasts because discoveries of new, rare, or out-of-range plants may more easily be made there.

Alvar is an extensive area of flat limestone pavement essentially at the earth's surface. A recent magazine article on alvars (*Wildflower*, Summer 1996) asserts that it is one of the rarer environments on our planet. Much of the world's alvar is located in Ontario, Canada, especially on the Bruce Peninsula and Manitoulin Island. Smaller amounts can be found in Michigan, on Drummond Island and in the Upper Peninsula, and in the Marblehead region near Toledo, Ohio.

Alvar, somewhat resembling a concrete-paved field, is essentially flat topography riddled with crevices, rock fractures, and occasionally deep fissures dissolved over time by acid waters that enlarge crevices. Mostly very dry and subject to day and night cycles of heating and drying followed by rapid cooling, the alvar is hostile to many plants. On its surface, concavities may support temporary or permanent pools of water, but these are infrequent. In places, accumulations of humus and soil particles may range from a fraction of an inch to many inches deep. In deeper accumulations of such soil, herbs, shrubs, even trees, sometimes stunted and elfin, may form conspicuous islands on the bare rock. On those "islands," plants may or may not be specialized for the dry rock conditions. On Manitoulin Island, such

"islands," surrounded by the dry alvar plants or bare rock, support White Cedar, Canada Fir, and spruce trees plus abundant colonies of lady's-slippers, Calypso, and Wood Lilies.

Many true alvar plants, however, must be able to withstand rapid change from wet to dry and prolonged summer dry spells. Crevices and fissures collect more humus, soil, and moisture, presenting a more favorable habitat for many plants. Where these abound, one may encounter rock crevice ferns and plants that do not occur elsewhere on the alvar. Many of the alvar plants occur in other habitats as well – prairies,

old fields, sand plains. But some specialize and occur in our region mainly on alvars. One species, Lakeside Daisy (*Hymenoxys herbacea*), was just recently discovered in Michigan. It occurs today only in one or two localities in the United States and a few in Canada – on alvars and alvar-like soils adjacent to the Great Lakes.

Some of our finest alvars have been severely disturbed or the native flora damaged by limestone quarrying and industrial mining.

Alleghany Vine; Climbing Fumitory
Adlumia fungosa
Fumitory Family

Alleghany Vine can be easily identified as the only vining plant in our area with typical "bleeding heart" flowers. Clambering over other vegetation by means of tendrils, this vine can be several feet long. Flowering occurs from June to October, the delicate, drooping white or purplish blossoms with united petals forming elongated "hearts."

A biennial or monocarpic plant, Alleghany Vine occurs on limestone outcrops, calcareous dunes, and some sandy soils. Rare but occasionally sometimes locally abundant on Great Lakes islands, it seems to thrive on recently disturbed soils in old cedar blowdowns or rock slides, perhaps needing periodic disturbance of seeds in the soil bank to stimulate germination.

Within its range, from Quebec and Ontario to Minnesota and New England south along the mountains to North Carolina and Tennessee, some occurrences may be introductions rather than native as Alleghany Vine was used widely as a garden plant in pioneer times.

fwc

Mountain Clematis
Clematis occidentalis
Buttercup Family

This long-lived vine holds the distinction of being our only native clematis with large, colorful sepals. As a member of the Buttercup Family, Mountain Clematis has no petals, the sepals attracting pollinators. Pale lavender to medium purple in color, they are 2 to 3 inches in length and somewhat drooping. Blooming in May and early June, the flowers occur on woody stems having 3-parted opposite or whorled leaves. Somewhat curly heads of fluffy seeds follow the flowers in mid-summer.

Mountain Clematis is found in light shade or sun, primarily on rocky outcrops, ledges, or rock slides. Although widely distributed from the Blue Ridge of Virginia and North Carolina north into eastern Canada, in our region it occurs locally in the western Upper Peninsula of Michigan, along the north shore of Lake Superior, and in northern Wisconsin and Minnesota only. In the latter location it also grows in aspen groves and thickets.

fwc

fwc

Mossy Stonecrop
Sedum acre
Orpine Family

An introduction from Europe, Mossy Stonecrop is becoming a dominant groundcover on the alvars of Manitoulin Island and elsewhere in the Great Lakes. Its succulent stems and leaves form dense evergreen carpets over rocks and other open, dry sites, often invading lawns. These verdant mats become yellow in June and July when small, starry, yellow flowers appear in branched clusters.

Mossy Stonecrop has established a wide range that includes the northernmost United States and adjacent Canada. Frequently used for rock gardens and cemetery plantings, it has spread extensively and is diffcult to eradicate.

Fragile Prickly-pear
Opuntia fragilis
Cactus Family

Another rare species in our area, Fragile Prickly-pear occurs on granite outcrops in the Huron Mountains where it may have been introduced by Native Americans. It becomes more frequent in a variety of habitats west of our coverage area and is the most northern of our native cacti, occurring in western Canada south to Arizona.

Almost round in cross-section, the stem segments of this cactus species lie on the ground with ends upturned. The segments break away from the plant readily, sometimes starting new plants and other times adhering to exposed clothing. Easily distinguishable from our other native cactus by its small, cylindrical stem segments, Fragile Prickly-pear produces showy yellow flowers in summer.

Lakeside Daisy
Hymenoxys herbacea
Aster or Daisy Family

One of the rarest plants in North America, Lakeside Daisy is classified as an endangered species in both the United States and Canada. Its only known occurences today are in the Marblehead region of Ohio, on the Bruce Peninsula and Manitoulin Island, and in Upper Michigan where a single new colony was recently discovered. Quarrying of limestone in its current habitats constitutes a severe threat to this species.

The narrow leaves of this plant are all basal. Occurring in slightly fleshy tufts that form dense mats, they have a single vein and glandular dots visible under magnification. Flowering stems achieve heights of 8 to 10 inches, bearing solitary, showy yellow daisies 1 to 2 inches in diameter in June.

Upland White Goldenrod; Sneezewort Goldenrod
Solidago ptarmicoides
Aster or Daisy Family

Stiff, leathery leaves enable Upland White Goldenrod to survive in extreme habitats such as calcareous rock outcrops and cliffs, although it occurs in other habitats as well. Misclassified until recently as an aster, this plant can reach heights up to 3 feet, but without competition for light from other plants, as in this setting, it remains short. The flat-topped inflorescence of aster-like flowers is borne on stems having erect, linear-lanceolate leaves. With blossoms characterized by 12 to 18 white ray flowers, it blooms from June to August, ahead of most of its family.

Typically found in small clumps, Upland White Goldenrod occurs from Quebec to Saskatchewan south to Vermont, New York, southern Ontario, northern Ohio and Indiana, Missouri, South Dakota, and Colorado. In our area, it is especially evident along the rocky shores of Lake Superior.

Three-toothed Cinquefoil
Potentilla tridentata
Rose Family

Three-toothed Cinquefoil occupies a variety of habitats including sandy barrens and bluffs and Jack Pine forest, but it is at its best on rocky outcrops where the plants produce dense clumps of leaves and flowers that follow crevices and seams in the rocks. Usually under 4 inches tall, the stems are somewhat woody with glossy, leathery, 3-parted leaves, each leaflet displaying 3 teeth at its tip. The branched flower stems grow 6 to 12 inches tall, bearing groups of small, 5-petaled white flowers from late May to October, but primarily in June and July. Densely hairy, hard, dry seeds follow the flowers.

252

fwc

Butterwort
Pinguicula vulgaris
Bladderwort Family

Butterwort has been previously discussed in the chapter on Great Lakes Shorelines and Dunes. But in the upper Great Lakes region, it occurs not only on wet sands and dune flats but also on mossy rocks. Large colonies of Butterwort can be found on wet seepages of Pictured Rocks, at high splash levels of Lake Superior breakers, and in the crevices of almost any kind of rock where the star-shaped clusters of slimy leaves (*pinguis* means oily or greasy) remotely resemble stranded starfish at low tide. Found inland only rarely in our region, around St. Ignace for example, Butterwort is common in the Arctic where it is called Tundra Violet.

Lingonberry; Mountain-cranberry
Vaccinium vitis-idaea
Heath Family

Also known as Mountain-cranberry, this shrubby creeper forms extensive patches that can cover acres. The lustrous, leathery, evergreen leaves of Lingonberry provide a show in themselves against the rocks, but this species presents its most striking face in flower and in fruit. The white or usually pink blossoms form in terminal clusters, their 4-parted petals united into a tiny bell. The bright red fruits, smaller than those of the related commercial cranberry and less acidic, become milder following exposure to winter weather.

Varying forms of Lingonberry occur worldwide in northern districts. Our Great Lakes form is smaller with smaller leaves than its Alaskan and European counterparts. More common on the north shores of Lake Superior, it is known in the Great Lakes States today only on Isle Royale and in northern Wisconsin and Minnesota. Within the United States, Lingonberry can also be found in Maine, New Hampshire, and the New England mountains. A larger European form has been introduced for horticultural purposes.

Lime-encrusted Saxifrage
Saxifraga paniculata
Saxifrage Family

Lime-encrusted Saxifrage forms clusters of hen-and-chicks-like leaf rosettes. Dotted with whitish lime secretions, the leaves are firm, leathery, and more or less toothed. Erect flower stems can be up to 18 inches tall, bearing a few alternate leaves. The white-petaled flowers occur in a branched panicle, the petals usually displaying red dots.

At our latitude, Lime-encrusted Saxifrage is rare and local. Known only from Minnesota's north shore of Lake Superior in our region, where it grows on outcroppings of basic rocks, it prefers north-facing exposures and bright but not direct sunlight.

Appendices

Appendix 1
Latin Names of Families

Common Family Name	Latin Family Name
Acanthus	Acanthaceae
Arum	Araceae
Aster or Daisy	Compositae (Asteraceae)
Barberry	Berberidaceae
Bellflower	Campanulaceae
Birthwort	Aristolochiaceae
Bladderwort	Lentibulariaceae
Borage	Boraginaceae
Broom-rape	Orobanchaceae
Buckbean	Menyanthaceae
Bur-reed	Sparganiaceae
Buttercup	Ranunculaceae
Cactus	Cactaceae
Carrot or Parsley	Umbelliferae (Apiaceae)
Cashew	Anacardiaceae
Cat-tail	Typhaceae
Dodder	Cuscutaceae
Dogwood	Cornaceae
Evening-primrose	Onagraceae
Flowering-rush	Butomaceae
Fumitory	Fumairiaceae
Gentian	Gentianaceae
Geranium	Gentianaceae
Ginseng	Araliaceae
Goosefoot	Chenopodiaceae
Gourd	Cucurbitaceae
Grass	Gramineae (Poaceae)
Heath	Ericaceae
Holly	Aquifoliaceae
Honeysuckle	Caprifoliaceae
Indian-pipe	Monotropaceae
Iris	Iridaceae
Lily	Liliaceae
Loosestrife	Lythraceae
Madder	Rubiaceae
Mallow	Malvaceae
Melastome	Melastomataceae
Milkweed	Asclepiadaceae
Milkwort	Polygalaceae
Mint	Labiatae
Morning-glory	Convolvulaceae
Mustard	Cruciferae (Brassicaceae)
Mustard	Urticaceae
Nettle	Solanaceae
Nightshade	Orchidaceae
Orchid	Crassulaceae
Pea	Leguminosae (Fabaceae)

Phlox	Polemoniaceae
Pickerel-weed	Pontideriaceae
Pink	Caryophyllaceae
Pitcher-plant	Sarraceniaceae
Poppy	Papaveraceae
Primrose	Primulaceae
Purslane	Portulacaceae
Rockrose	Cistaceae
Rose	Rosaceae
Saxifrage	Saxifragaceae
Sedge	Cyperaceae
Shinleaf or Wintergreen	Pyrolaceae
Smartweed	Polygonaceae
Snapdragon	Scrophulariaceae
Spiderwort	Commelinaceae
Spurge	Euphorbiaceae
St. John's-wort	Guttiferae (Clusiaceae)
Sundew	Droseraceae
Teasel	Dipsacaceae
Touch-me-not	Balsaminaceae
Violet	Violaceae
Water-lily	Nymphaeaceae
Water-plantain	Alismataceae
Waterleaf	Hydrophyllaceae

Appendix 2
Species List by Color

The following list is included as an aid to identfication of wildflowers in their natural habitats. For purposes of simplicity, all species are grouped within seven basic color families according to their most common and/or predominant color. Readers should remember, however, that variations within a single color family can be great, and many species occur in more than one color.

Pink
(including rose, magenta, and orchid)

Alleghany Vine; Climbing Fumitory	*Adlumia fungosa*
Arethusa; Dragon's Mouth	*Arethusa bulbosa*
Common Milkweed	*Asclepias syriaca*
Flowering-rush	*Butomus umbellatus*
Grass-pink	*Calopogon tuberosus*
Calypso; Fairy-slipper	*Calypso bulbosa*
Pink Spring Cress	*Cardamine douglassii*
Pipsissewa; Prince's-pine	*Chimaphila umbellata*
Broad-leaved Spring-beauty	*Claytonia caroliniana*
Narrow-leaved Spring-beauty	*Claytonia virginica*
Pink Lady's-slipper	*Cypripedium acaule*
Showy Lady's-slipper; Queen's Lady's-slipper	*Cypripedium reginae*
Shooting-star	*Dodecatheon meadia*
Purple Coneflower	*Echinacea pallida*
Fireweed; Great Willow-herb	*Epilobium angustifolium*
Common Fleabane	*Erigeron philadelphicus*
Queen-of-the-prairie	*Filipendula rubra*
Prairie Smoke; Prairie Avens	*Geum triflorum*
Rose Mallow; Swamp Mallow	*Hibiscus moscheutos*
Sheep-laurel, Lambkill	*Kalmia angustifolia*
Pale- or Bog-laurel	*Kalmia polifolia*
Twinflower	*Linnaea borealis*
Musk Mallow	*Malva moschata*
Wild-bergamot	*Monarda fistulosa*
Prairie Phlox	*Phlox pilosa*
False Dragonhead; Obedient Plant	*Physostegia virginiana*
Rose Pogonia	*Pogonia ophioglossoides*
Willow-weed, Nodding Smartweed	*Polygonum lepathifolium*
Water Smartweed	*Polygonum amphibium*
Pink Shinleaf	*Pyrola asarifolia*
Meadow-beauty; Deergrass	*Rhexia virginica*
Common Marsh-pink; Rose-pink; Rose Gentian	*Sabatia angularis*
Red Clover	*Trifolium pratense*
Common Cranberry; Large Cranberry	*Vaccinium macrocarpon*
Lingonberry; Mountain Cranberry	*Vaccinium vitis-idea*

White
(inlcuding cream and tan)

White Baneberry; Doll's-eyes	*Actaea pachypoda*
Red Baneberry	*Actaea rubra*
Wild Leek; Ramps	*Allium tricoccum*
Beach Grass	*Ammophila breviligulata*
Canada Anemone	*Anemone canadensis*
Flat-topped Aster	*Aster umbellatus*
White or Prairie False Indigo	*Baptisia lactea*
Wild Calla; Water-arum	*Calla palustris*
Low Bindweed	*Calystegia spithamaea*
Buttonbush	*Cephalanthes occidentalis*
Turtlehead	*Chelone glabra*
Pitcher's or Dune Thistle	*Cirsium pitcheri*
Virgin's Bower; Woodbine	*Clematis virginiana*
Bunchberry; Canada Dogwood	*Cornus canadensis*
Common Dodder; Swamp Dodder	*Cuscuta gronovii*
Wild Carrot; Queen-Anne's-lace	*Daucus carota*
Two-leaved Toothwort	*Dentaria diphylla*
Squirrel-corn	*Dicentra canadensis*
Dutchman's-breeches	*Dicentra cucullaria*
Shooting-star	*Dodecatheon meadia*
Round-leaved Sundew	*Drosera rotundifolia*
Narrow-leaved Sundew	*Drosera intermedia*
Wild-cucumber	*Echinocystis lobata*
Trailing-arbutus	*Epigaea repens*
Cotton-grass; Bog-cotton	*Eriophorum viridi-carinatum*
Rattlesnake-master	*Eryngium yuccifolium*
White Trout-lily or Dogtooth-violet	*Erythronium albidum*
Boneset	*Eupatorium perfoliatum*
Flowering Spurge	*Euphorbia corollata*
Wintergreen; Teaberry	*Gaultheria procumbens*
White Closed or Bottle Gentian	*Gentiana andrewsii alba*
Downy Rattlesnake Plantain	*Goodyera pubescens*
Creeping Rattlesnake Plantain	*Goodyera repens*
Sharp-lobed Hepatica	*Hepatica acutiloba*
Goldenseal	*Hydrastis canadensis*
Virginia Waterleaf	*Hydrophyllum virginianum*
Twinleaf	*Jeffersonia diphylla*
Labrador-tea	*Ledum groenlandicum*
Canada Mayflower	*Maianthemum canadense*
Buckbean	*Menyanthes trifoliata*
Partridge-berry	*Mitchella repens*
Bishop's-cap	*Mitella diphylla*
One-flowered Shinleaf	*Moneses uniflora*
Indian-pipe	*Monotropa uniflora*
Fragrant Water Lily	*Nymphaea odorata*
Dwarf Ginseng	*Panax trifolius*
Lousewort	*Pedicularis canadensis*
Foxglove Beard-tongue	*Penstemon digitalis*
White Fringed-orchid	*Platanthera blephariglottis*
Tall White Bog-orchid; Bog-candle	*Platanthera diltata*
Eastern Prairie Fringed-orchid	*Platanthera leucophaea*
May-apple	*Podophyllum peltatum*
Three-toothed Cinquefoil	*Potentilla tridentata*
Common Blackberry	*Rubus alleganiensis*

Thimbleberry	*Rubus parviflorus*
Wild Red Raspberry	*Rubus strigosus*
Wapato; Duck-potato	*Sagittaria latifolia*
Bloodroot	*Sanguinaria canadensis*
Bouncing Bet	*Saponaria officinalis*
Lime-encrusted Saxifrage	*Saxifraga paniculata*
False Spikenard	*Smilacina racemosa*
False Soloman-seal	*Smilacina stellata*
Three-leaved False Soloman-seal	*Smilacina trifolia*
Gray Goldenrod	*Solidago nemoralis*
Upland White or Sneezewort Goldenrod	*Solidago ptarmacoides*
Bur-reed	*Sparganium eurycarpum*
Goats-rue; Rabbit-pea	*Tephrosia virginiana*
Foamflower; False Miterwort	*Tiarella cordifolia*
False Asphodel; Sticky Tofieldia	*Tofieldia glutinosa*
Star-flower	*Trientalis borealis*
Common Trillium	*Trillium grandiflorum*
Snow Trillium	*Trillium nivale*
Highbush Blueberry	*Vaccinium corymbosum*
Culver's Root	*Veronicastrum virginicum*
Canada Violet	*Viola canadensis*

Blue
(including violet, purple, lavender, and reddish purple)

Wild-ginger	*Asarum canadense*
Purple Milkweed	*Ascelpias purpurescens*
Swamp Milkweed	*Asclepias incarnata*
New England Aster	*Aster nova-angliae*
Harebell; Bluebell	*Campanula rotundifolia*
Star-thistle; Spotted Knapweed	*Centaurea maculosa*
Chicory	*Cichorium intybus*
Bull Thistle	*Cirsium vulgare*
Swamp Thistle	*Cirsium muticum*
Mountain Clematis	*Clematis occidentalis*
Blue-eyed Mary	*Collinsia verna*
Beggar's-tick; Canada Tick-trefoil	*Desmodium canadense*
Teasel	*Dipsacus fullonum*
Viper's Bugloss; Blueweed	*Echium vulgare*
Joe-pye-weed	*Eupatorium maculatum*
Closed or Bottle Gentian	*Gentiana andrewsii*
Prairie Gentian	*Gentiana puberalenta*
Fringed Gentian	*Gentianopsis procera*
Wild Geranium; Crane's-bill	*Geranium maculatum*
Broad-leaved or Canada Waterleaf	*Hydrophyllum canadense*
Dwarf Lake Iris	*Iris lacustris*
Wild Blue Flag; Wild Iris	*Iris versicolor*
Beach Pea	*Lathyrus maritimus*
Rough Blazing-star	*Liatris aspera*
Blazing-star	*Liatris spicata*
Great Blue Lobelia	*Lobelia siphilitica*
Wild Lupine	*Lupinus perennis*
Purple Loosestrife	*Lythrum salicaria*
Virginia "Bluebells" or Cowslip	*Mertensia virginica*
Forget-me-not	*Myosotis scorpioides*
Broom-rape; Cancer-root	*Orobanche uniflora*
Sand Phlox	*Phlox bifida*

263

Wild Blue Phlox	*Phlox divaricata*
Butterwort	*Pinguicula vulgaris*
Small Purple Fringed-orchid	*Platanthera psycodes*
Flowering- wintergreen	*Polygala paucifolia*
Fringed Polygala	*Polygala paucifolia*
Pickerel-weed	*Pontederia cordata*
Ruellia; Wild-petunia	*Ruellia humilis*
Blue-eyed Grass	*Sisyrinchium angustifolium*
Spiderwort	*Tradescantia ohiensis*
Spiderwort	*Tradescantia virginiana*
Prairie Trillium; Toadshade	*Trillium recurvatum*
Toadshade; Sessile Trillium	*Trillium sessile*
Missouri Ironweed	*Vernonia missurica*
Hairy Vetch	*Vicia villosa*
Birdfoot Violet	*Viola pedata*
Long-spurred Violet	*Viola rostrata*
Common or Woolly Blue Violet	*Viola sororia*

Red
(including scarlet, bright red, medium red, and orange)

Red Anemone	*Anemone multifida*
Wild Columbine	*Aquilegia canadensis*
Purple Milkweed	*Ascelpias purpurescens*
Butterfly-weed	*Asclepias tuberosa*
Indian Paintbrush	*Castilleja coccinea*
Striped Coral-root	*Corallorhiza striata*
Orange Hawkweed	*Hieracium aurantiacum*
Spotted Touch-me-not	*Impatiens capensis*
Michigan Lily; Turk-cap Lily	*Lilium michiganense*
Cardinal Flower; Red Lobelia	*Lobelia cardinalis*

Dark Red
(including maroon, brownish red, and brown)

Groundnut; Wild-bean	*Apios americana*
Wild Ginger	*Asarum canadense*
Spotted Coral-root	*Corallorhiza maculata*
Ram's-head Lady's-Slipper	*Cypripedium arietinum*
Pine-drops	*Pterospora andromedea*
Skunk-cabbage	*Symplocarpus foetidus*
Stinking Benjamin; Wake-robin	*Trillium erectum*

Green

Green Dragon; Dragon-root	*Arisaema dracontium*
Jack-in-the-pulpit	*Arisaema triphyllum*
Strawberry Blite	*Chenopodium capitatum*
Common Water-hemlock	*Cicuta maculata*
American Columbo	*Frasera carolinensis*
Downy Rattlesnake Plantain	*Goodyera pubescens*
Michigan Holly; Winterberry	*Ilex verticillata*
Naked Miterwort	*Mitella nuda*
Horse Mint; Spotted Bergamot	*Monarda punctata*
Green Shinleaf; Pyrola	*Pyrola chlorantha*
Staghorn Sumac	*Rhus typhina*
Poison Sumac	*Toxicodendron vernix*
Narrow-leaved Cat-tail	*Typha angustifolia*

Common Cat-tail	*Typha latifolia*
White Camas; Death Camas	*Zigadenus glaucus*
Wild-rice	*Zizania aquatica*

Yellow

Smooth False Foxglove	*Aureolaria flava*
Yellow Rocket	*Barbarea vulgaris*
Nodding Beggar-ticks; Stick-tight; Nodding Bur-marigold	*Bidens cernuus*
Marsh-marigold; Cowslip	*Caltha palustris*
Bluebead-lily; Corn-lily	*Clintonia borealis*
Squaw-root	*Conopholis americana*
Sand Coreopsis; Long-stalked Tickseed	*Coreopsis lanceolata*
Small Yellow Lady's-slipper	*Cypripedium parviflorum*
Large Yellow Lady's-slipper	*Cypripedium parviflorum var. pubescens*
Yellow Trout-lily or Dogtooth-violet	*Erythronium americanum*
Common Sneezeweed	*Helenium autumnale*
Frostweed; Rockrose	*Helianthemum canadense*
Downy Sunflower	*Helianthus mollis*
Yellow Hawkweed; King Devil	*Hieracium piloselloides*
Sand Heather; Beach-heath; False Heather	*Hudsonia tomentosa*
Lakeside Daisy	*Hymenoxys herbacea*
Kalm's St. John's-wort	*Hypericum kalmianum*
Common St. John's-wort	*Hypericum perforatum*
Star-grass	*Hypoxis hirsuta*
Yellow Flag	*Iris pseudacorus*
Butter-and-eggs	*Linaria vulgaris*
Hairy or Yellow Puccoon	*Lithospermum carolinense*
Hoary Puccoon	*Lithospermum canescens*
False Loosestrife; Seedbox	*Ludwigia alternifolia*
Fringed Loosestrife	*Lysimachia ciliata*
Tufted Loosestrife	*Lysimachia thyrsiflora*
Yellow Sweet-clover	*Melilotus officinalis*
American Lotus	*Nelumbo lutea*
Pond-lily; Cow-lily; Spatterdock	*Nuphar variegata*
Evening-primrose	*Oenothera biennis*
Sundrops	*Oenothera perennis*
Fragile Prickly-pear	*Opuntia fragilis*
Prickly-pear	*Opuntia humifusa*
Lousewort	*Pedicularis canadensis*
Yellow Fringed-orchid	*Platanthera ciliaris*
Silverweed	*Potentilla anserina*
Shrubby Cinquefoil	*Potentilla fruticosa*
Yellow Water Crowfoot	*Ranunculus flabellaris*
Swamp Buttercup	*Ranunculus hispidus*
Prairie Coneflower; Yellow Coneflower	*Ratibida pinnata*
Black-eyed Susan	*Rudbeckia hirta*
Tall or Cutleaf Coneflower	*Rudbeckia laciniata*
Mossy Stonecrop	*Sedum acre*
Golden Ragwort	*Senecio aureus*
Prairie Rosin-weed	*Silphium integrifolium*
Compass Plant; Rosin-weed	*Silphium lacinatum*
Cup-plant	*Silphium perfoliatum*
Prairie-dock	*Silphium terebinthinaceum*
Early Goldenrod	*Solidago juncea*
Gray Goldenrod	*Solidago nemoralis*

Riddell's Goldenrod	*Solidago ridellii*
Showy Goldenrod	*Solidago speciosa*
Slender Ladies'-tresses	*Spiranthes lacera*
Lake Huron Tansy	*Tanacetum huronense*
Goat's-beard; Vegetable Oyster; Salsify	*Tragopogon dubius*
Flat-leaved Bladderwort	*Utricula intermedia*
Horned Bladderwort	*Utricularia cornuta*
Bellwort	*Uvularia grandiflora*
Common Mullein	*Verbascum phlomoides*
Mullein	*Verbascum thapsus*
Yellow Violet	*Viola pubescens*
Golden Alexanders	*Zizia aurea*

Drawings of Plant Parts

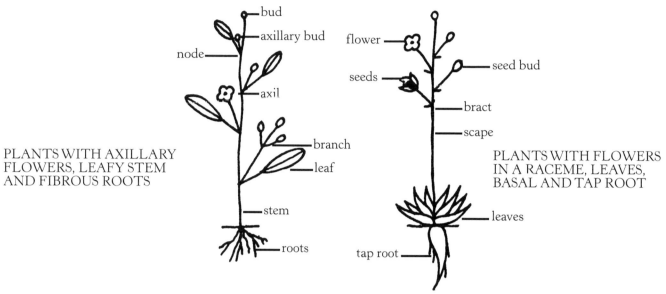

PLANTS WITH AXILLARY
FLOWERS, LEAFY STEM
AND FIBROUS ROOTS

bud

axillary bud

node

axil

branch

leaf

stem

roots

flower

seeds

seed bud

bract

scape

leaves

tap root

PLANTS WITH FLOWERS
IN A RACEME, LEAVES,
BASAL AND TAP ROOT

PLANTS AND THEIR PARTS

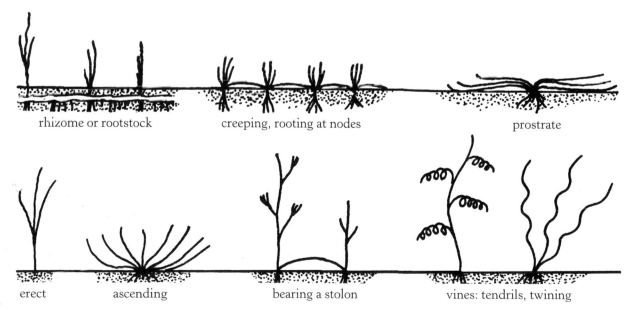

rhizome or rootstock

creeping, rooting at nodes

prostrate

erect

ascending

bearing a stolon

vines: tendrils, twining

GROWTH PATTERNS OF STEMS

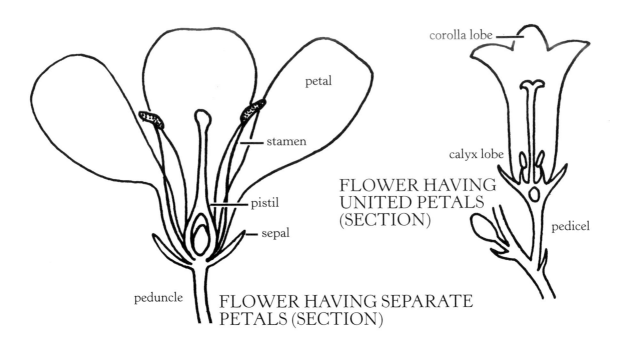

petal

stamen

pistil

sepal

peduncle

FLOWER HAVING SEPARATE
PETALS (SECTION)

corolla lobe

calyx lobe

FLOWER HAVING
UNITED PETALS
(SECTION)

pedicel

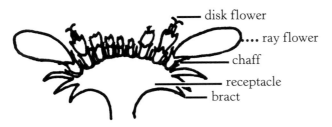

disk flower

ray flower

chaff

receptacle

bract

HEAD OF COMPOSITE
INFLORESCENCE
(SECTION)

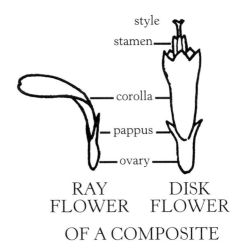

style

stamen

corolla

pappus

ovary

RAY
FLOWER

DISK
FLOWER

OF A COMPOSITE

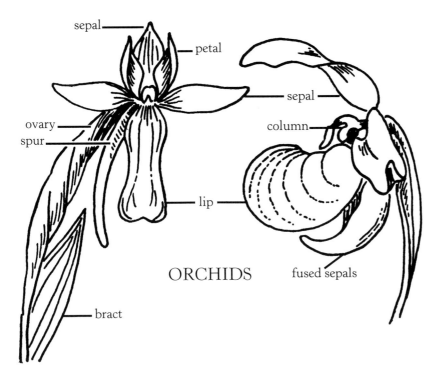

sepal

petal

ovary

spur

lip

sepal

column

fused sepals

ORCHIDS

bract

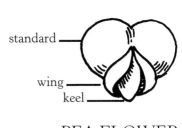

standard

wing

keel

PEA FLOWER

corolla regular, petals separate

corolla irregular, petals separate

petals united

corolla irregular, 2-lipped

-with spur

COROLLA TYPES

tubular

bell-shaped (campanulate)

un-shaped

funnel-shaped

COROLLA TYPES, all regular, petals united

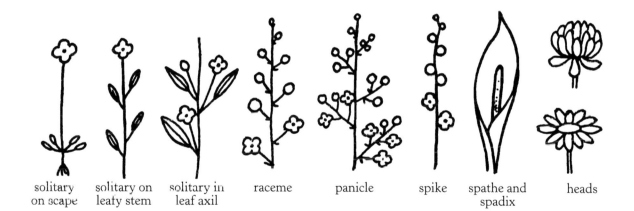

solitary on scape

solitary on leafy stem

solitary in leaf axil

raceme

panicle

spike

spathe and spadix

heads

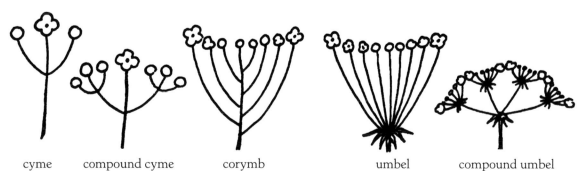

cyme

compound cyme

corymb

umbel

compound umbel

INFLORESCENCE TYPES

269

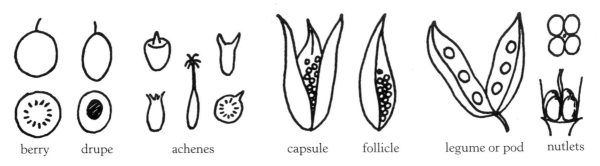

berry   drupe   achenes   capsule   follicle   legume or pod   nutlets

FRUIT TYPES

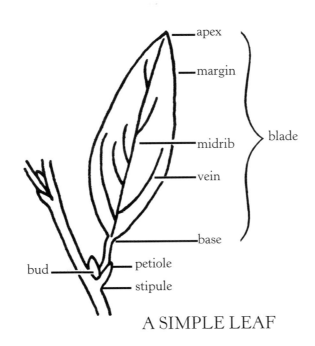

A SIMPLE LEAF

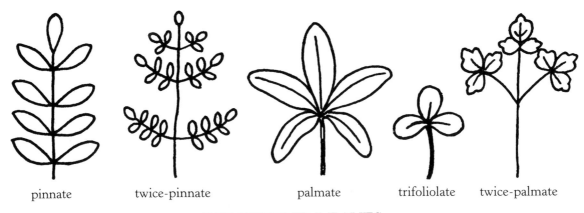

pinnate   twice-pinnate   palmate   trifoliolate   twice-palmate

COMPOUND LEAVES

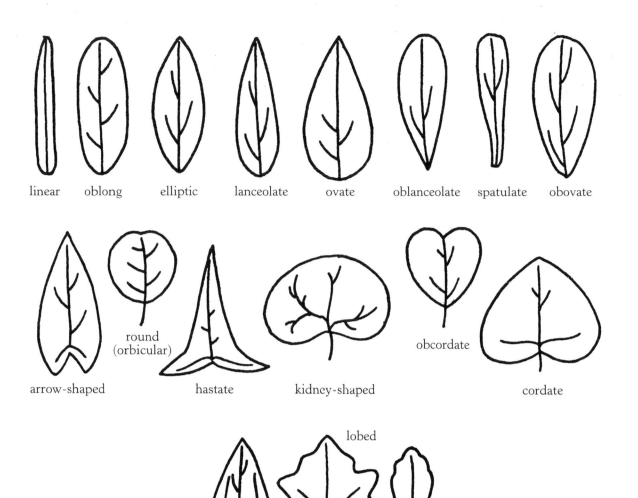

linear   oblong   elliptic   lanceolate   ovate   oblanceolate   spatulate   obovate

arrow-shaped   round (orbicular)   hastate   kidney-shaped   obcordate   cordate

lobed

palmate   parted

LEAF SHAPES

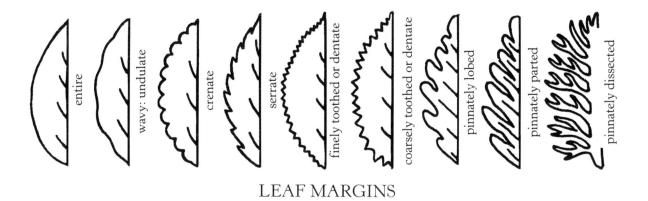

entire   wavy: undulate   crenate   serrate   finely toothed or dentate   coarsely toothed or dentate   pinnately lobed   pinnately parted   pinnately dissected

LEAF MARGINS

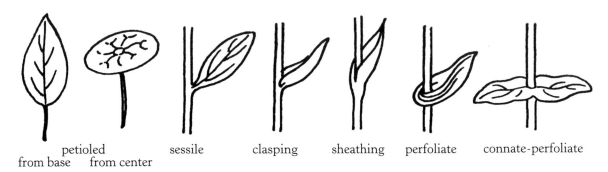

petioled
from base   from center   sessile   clasping   sheathing   perfoliate   connate-perfoliate

LEAF ATTACHMENTS

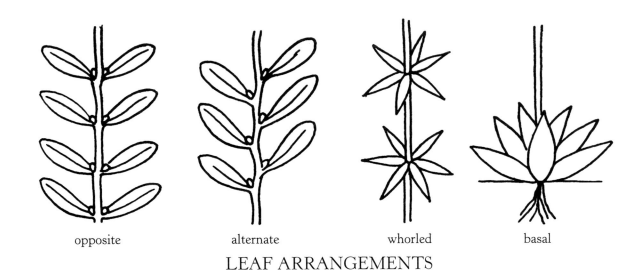

opposite   alternate   whorled   basal

LEAF ARRANGEMENTS

272

Glossary

Alkaline	Basic or non-acid pH; applied to certain soils among other things.
Alkaloid	Organic substance of alkaline properties, particularly those occurring in plants and animals.
Alluvial soil	Soil deposited by running water.
Alvar	Flat limestone rock ("pavement") with shallow or no soil and with usually grassy vegetation.
Annual	A plant that germinates, flowers, and sets seed in a single growing season.
Anther	The pollen-bearing part of a stamen.
Axil	The angle at which a leaf or branch joins a stem or main axis.
Barren or barrens	An area which, for whatever reasons, has sparse, often stunted plant growth.
Basal	At the base of the plant or at ground level.
Biennial	A plant that lives for two years, often producing a rosette of leaves the first year and a flowering stem the second.
Bilaterally symmetrical	Capable of division into mirror-image halves on only one plane.
Biome (Biota)	A major climax community composed of plants and animals.
Bog	An undrained wetland with strongly acid, mineral-poor soil (usually peat). In the strictest sense, true bogs are not forested. Some biologists refer to forested acid peatlands as "treed bogs," often naming the dominant trees as in "Black Spruce-Tamarack bog."
Boreal	Northern.
Bract	A reduced, leaf-like, sometimes scale-like structure often below a flower, pedicel, or branch.
Bulb	A short underground shoot that bears fleshy overlapping leaves (as in an onion).
Calcareous	Limy; rich in calcium carbonates as limestone or marl.
Calyx	The collective sepals of a single flower.
Capsule	A fruit that splits open along two or more lines or joints, usually several- or many-seeded.
Carnivorous	Meat-eating; said of plants that trap insects and digest them. Such plants are also termed insectivorous.
Carr	See *Karr*.
Chlorophyll	The green coloring matter in plants that absorbs light energy and builds a glucose molecule, a part of the process of photosynthesis.
Circumboreal	Occurring around the world in northern regions.
Cleft	Deeply cut.
Cleistogamous	(Of a flower) fertilized and setting seed without opening.
Climax formation	A relatively stable, enduring plant formation that results from a long series of successional changes.
Climax vegetation	The plants of a given climax formation.
Clone	All of the individuals derived asexually from a single sexually produced organism; hence, all plants of the clone are genetically identical.

Compound	Composed of more than one part or branched, as a leaf with several leaflets.
Contractile	Capable of contracting.
Corm	A short, thick, condensed, underground stem lacking the fleshy leaves that characterize a bulb.
Corolla	The petals, collectively, of a single flower.
Corona	A crown of inner petal-like appendages.
Crown	An inner appendage to a petal or to the throat of the corolla.
Deciduous	(Of leaves) falling off naturally at the end of the growing season; (of floral parts) shed readily.
Declining stems	Stems bent or turned slightly downward.
Dioecious	Having the sexes on separate plants.
Discrete	Separate, distinct.
Disjunct	Occurring in two or more separated geographical areas.
Disk flower	In the Composite Family, the portion of the flower head consisting of radially symmetrical flowers in a solid central mass.
Diurnal	Daily; occurring in the daytime.
Doctrine of Signatures	An ancient belief that the creator provided hints as to the medicinal usage of plants in their markings or the shapes of their parts, i.e. the Sharp-lobed Hepatica with its three-lobed leaf shaped similarly to the human liver was thought to be useful in treating liver ailments.
Drupe	A non-splitting fleshy fruit with the seed (or seeds) enclosed in a hard tissue forming one or more central pits.
Dune	A crescent-shaped sand hill formed by windblown sand.
Elliptic	Longer than wide, broadest at the middle, and tapering almost equally toward both ends.
Emergent vegetation	Plants rooted in the soil beneath water and reaching up to produce leaves and flowers in the air above.
Ephemeral	Lasting for a short time (of flower parts, less than a day).
Fen	A wetland with obstructed or weak drainage having mineral-rich, calcareous, neutral to alkaline soil. Peat, if present, is mineral-rich and non-acid. In its strictest sense, a fen is without trees and dominated by grasses and sedges. If trees develop on the site it becomes a "treed fen."
Fen seep	A seepage area in a fen.
Filament	The stalk of a stamen.
Forest Canopy	The uppermost layer of vegetation covering an area. There can be several layers of plants of varying heights on a given sight.
Fruit	A ripened ovary of a flower and any closely associated structures.
Genus	A group of similar species forming a unit structurally distinct from other groups of species.
Glaucous	Covered with a pale waxy coating or "bloom."
Glochid	A barbed hair or bristle.
Habitat	The type of environment in which a particular species occurs.
Hemiparasite	Attached to a host plant but also having the capacity for photosynthesis.
Herbaceous	A soft-tissued, non-woody plant.
Heterogeneous	Not uniform in kind.
Hoary	With fine gray or whitish hairs.

Hooded	Bearing a hood-like or covering structure (a cowl).
Humus	Decomposing leaf mold or other organic matter in the soil.
Hybrid	The offspring of dissimilar parents, especially parents of two different species.
Indirect parasite	An organism that utilizes an intermediate organism (usually a species of fungus) to connect to a host plant. The fungus obtains food from the host and passes it back to the original parasite.
Inflorescence	An entire flower cluster, including stalks and bracts; often used to cover clusters of fruit as well.
Karr, Carr, Shrub carr	A region dominated by shrub growth, often an early stage in wetland succession.
Keel	A ridge somewhat centrally located on the long axis of a structure such as a sepal.
Lacerated	Ragged, irregularly cleft, appearing as if torn.
Lacustrine	Belonging to or living in lakes.
Lagg	A moat that surrounds many domed or raised bogs.
Lanceolate	Narrow and elongate, broadest below the middle, lance-shaped.
Lichen	A growth of distinctive shape comprised of dual organisms, a dependent fungus and an independent photosynthetic partner, living together symbiotically.
Linear	Narrow and elongate with parallel sides.
Loam	In geology, soil of a definite particle size; in general usage, a friable, fertile soil.
Loment	A legume composed of 1-seeded articles.
Marl	A limy soil; in the northern regions, a deposit of white, clayey lime forming in lakes, streams, fens, and sometimes bogs.
Marsh	Treeless vegetation at least seasonally wet. A wet area with slow but definite drainage, usually with standing water and cat-tail or rush-like emergent vegetation and few or no trees.
Monocarpic	Blooming only once after maturity, then dying.
Mutant	An organism that bears a mutation (in genetics, the changed gene itself).
Mutation	A change in the DNA (gene) of an organism which, when occurring in reproductive cells, may be passed on to offspring.
Nectary	An organ that produces nectar.
Opposite	Two at a node and approximately 180° apart, as in some leaves.
Ovate	Shaped in general outline like a longitudinal section of an egg.
Panicle	An inflorescence in which the individual flower stalks arise from a branched axis rather than a simple central axis.
Parasitic	Dependent upon (and attached to) another plant for nutrition.
Patterned fen; patterned peatland	A peatland that has parallel raised ridges of peat and dwarfed vegetation alternating with pools of water.
Peat	Dead plant material, especially the remains of sphagnum mosses and associated vegetation, partially decomposing and accumulating underwater.
Pedicel	The stalk of an individual flower, spikelet, or head.
Perennial	A plant that will live indefinitely and, once mature, flower year after year provided the environment remains suitable.
Perfoliate	With the stem (or other stalk) appearing to pass through the leaf (or other blade).

Petal	One of the divisions of the corolla.
pH	The chemical symbol for the measurement of the hydrogen ion concentration of a substance which indicates its degree of acidity or alkalinity. Numbers below 7 indicate the acid condition; those above 7 the alkaline condition.
Photosynthesis	The process whereby chlorophyll-bearing organisms, mostly green plants, using water, carbon dioxide, and the energy of sunlight, create basic organic molecules (sugars) and release free oxygen into the atmosphere.
Pinnate	Arranged in 2 rows, one on each side of a common axis, as the pinna of a feather.
Pistil	One of the female or seed-producing structures of a flower.
Plant association	(As used herein) Groups of species that characteristically occur together within this region, not necessarily a category as used by plant ecologists.
Plant formation	An assemblage of plants essentially equivalent to a climax formation or biome.
Plant succession	The process of replacement of one plant community by another on a given site through competition and adaptational advantage until a stabilized climax is reached.
Pollen	The grains produced in the anther.
Pothole bog	A bog that develops in a pond or small lake in a glacial depression. Such bogs in their earlier stages usually show distinct zones of succession resembling a bull's-eye from above. These bogs occur as isolated islands of peatland plants south of the region where larger boreal patterned peatlands occur.
Prairie	A naturally treeless area drier than a marsh.
Propagule	Any structure possessed by an organism to increase the number of individuals, i.e. seed, spore, or runner.
Pubescent	With hairs (of whatever size or texture).
Quagmire	Very wet land unable to support the weight of any large organism, i.e. bog and quicksand.
Raceme	A type of inflorescence in which each flower is on an unbranched stalk attached to an unbranched elongate central axis.
Radially symmetrical	A body shape with equal parts radiating around a central axis, divisible into equal parts as in cutting a pie.
Ray flower	In the Composite Family, the ring or rings of outer flowers, each bearing a single, large, colorful petal.
Recurved	Curved downward or backward.
Reflexed	Bent back or downwards.
Relict	Localized plants evidently left over from past geological epochs.
Rhizome	An underground stem, usually somewhat elongate and growing horizontally (distinguishable from a root by the presence of nodes).
Rosette	A somewhat dense and circular cluster of leaves.
Saprophyte	A plant incapable of photosynthesis but not directly parasitic on any green plant (usually on a fungus).
Savanna	Vegetation consisting of grassland with trees scattered (not forming a closed canopy) or in scattered clumps.
Scape	A flower stalk arising from the base of the plant, i.e. from the root or rhizome, etc.
Sepal	One of the divisions of the calyx.
Sessile	Attached without a stalk.
Simple	Composed of a single or unbranched part; i.e. a leaf with one blade.

Shrub carr	See *Karr*.
Slack	A more or less linear depression between hills.
Slough	A swamp, bog, or marsh, especially one that is part of a backwater or inlet.
Spadix	An inflorescence consisting of small sessile flowers on a somewhat elongate fleshy axis.
Spathe	A single leaf-like structure (occasionally more) at the base of an inflorescence, often associated with the Arum Family.
Sphagnum	A genus of bog mosses that characteristically carpet bogs and many wetlands; a major producer of peat accumulations.
Spike	An elongated, unbranched inflorescence in which the flowers are sessile.
Spur	A hollow, sac-like or tubular extension of an organ.
Stamen	One of the male or pollen-producing structures of a flower, usually consisting of a filament and an anther.
Substrate	The surface or layer upon which a given plant grows, as in the soil on which a certain violet is found.
Swale	A natural (unlike a ditch), somewhat elongate depression, at least seasonally wet.
Swamp	A wooded area that is wet at least seasonally.
Symbiosis; symbiotic	Individuals of two different species living together for mutual benefit.
Tendrils	A slender coiling or twining organ, as on some vines.
Thyrse	A contracted, compact pannicle as in a cluster of grapes (see pannicle).
Tuffa	An extremely porous limestone precipitate that frequently forms in hillside springs and in regions of marl bog.
Umbel	An inflorescence in which the pedicels arise from the same point or nearly so.
Weed	An aggressive plant that grows where it is unwanted.
Whorl	A ring of 3 or more similar structures around a stem or other axis.
Wing	A thin expansion of tissue; a lateral petal, as in a pea flower.

Index

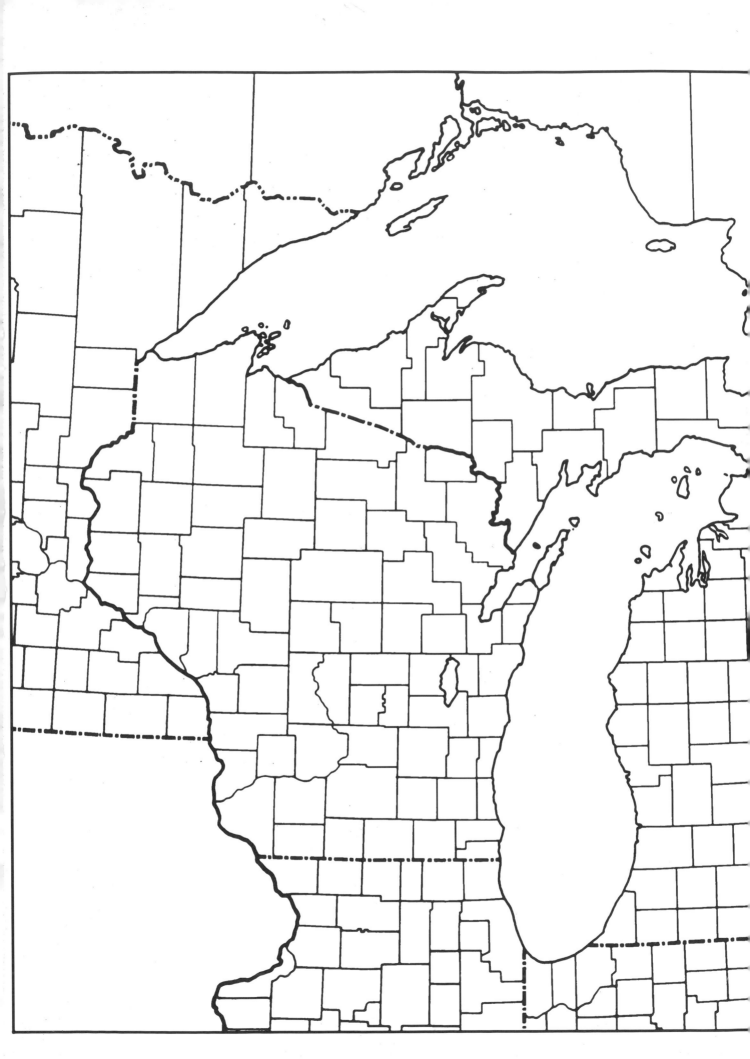